CHIEF EVERYTHING OFFICER

A FIELD GUIDE FOR SMALL ORGANISATION LEADERS

FLÓRA RAFFAI

CHIEF EVERYTHING OFFICER:
A FIELD GUIDE FOR SMALL ORGANISATION LEADERS

First Edition

ISBN: 978-1-4717-0285-3

Imprint: Lulu.com

"No one ever steps in the same river twice, for it's not the same river and they're not the same person."

– Heraclitus

CONTENTS

FOREWORD

I first became a CEO of a small organisation when I was 23. I was not prepared. I had not been mentored into the role or coached for many years prior to assuming the role and all of its responsibilities. I was two years into my first job and I was in the right place at the right time. I compensated for this lack of experience by developing a sizable imposter syndrome, reading all the management and leadership books recommended by others, and undertaking all of the (free - we had no budget) training I could find. I made a lot of mistakes; I learned from some of them. I changed jobs to lead a larger team and made fewer of the old mistakes and a bunch of new ones. I learned from more of them. I changed jobs again and I am still learning.

This book was originally written for myself as a collection of my key learnings from my seven years as a CEO. It was meant to be a reference point where I could look up a topic, remind myself of what I had learned, and then do better than I did the first time.

It is my hope that this book may also help you if you find yourself newly in the role of CEO at a small organisation. It does not need to be read cover to cover (although you are more than welcome to do so) - it is intended to be more of a field guide that you can dip in and out of depending on your need. The book is a summary of key information and advice based on my own experiences - there are many references to other books written by experts that go into much more depth on each topic that you can explore where you have the interest and the time.

I wish you the very best with your role. It is a challenging one, but fulfilling one.

INTRODUCTION

The role of a CEO

The role of a CEO is to develop and protect the team and the organisation. It is to smooth the way so everyone can do their jobs to the best of their abilities. It is to provide a vision, strategy, and direction for that work. It is to provide meaning. It is the role to lift everyone up and shield them when the shit hits the fan. Recognise and give credit, rather than taking it all for yourself. Hold the team accountable, whilst being ultimately accountable for the organisation.

The role of a CEO is to provide the structure and the parameters within which work is to take place. It is to define what 'great' looks like: the targets, the values, the behaviour, and the culture. To celebrate those that embody the values, and to guide or manage out those that do not. Where an organisation has a board, it is the CEO's role to work with it, take direction from the board, and translate board discussions into day-to-day actions.

The role of a CEO is not to know everything or to fix everything, however. It is to build an effective team and enable the team to solve their own problems. Remember, your team members often have a deeper understanding of each problem and the context, so they are in the best position to find the solution. The CEO's role is often to coach the team through the problem.

Finally, all successful CEOs are in their roles only because their teams and/or their boards believe in their ability to lead. CEOs are not intrinsically better than anyone else in their team; they are not of superior stock. All team members have specialist skills, a CEO is merely specialised in leadership. CEOs must maintain the respect and trust of their teams; CEOs are accountable and should act as the leading example of how all team members should act.

Do you want to be a CEO?

There are many perks associated with being the CEO. You tend to get paid well (at least in comparison to everyone else in the organisation), get good benefits, you tend to be treated with respect, your opinions are listened to and considered, you can shape the organisation into a place where you enjoy working, you get invited to interesting meetings and conferences, and so on.

There are also many downsides associated with being the CEO. You are ultimately responsible for everything, so you take on some degree of stress with every problem that takes place. You do not always get thought of as a person by team members as they can sometimes only see the role and the impact of the decisions you make. It is assumed you know everything and you will be expected to make decisions as if you do. When things go wrong, people expect you to fix it. Where things come up that are not on anyone's job description, it falls to you to do it - at least in a small organisation. Indeed, in a small organisation 'CEO' often stands for Chief Everything Officer as you plug all the gaps and wear all the hats. You are seen as the voice of the organisation, so you have to be extremely careful in what you say. People can be intimidated by you and so will not always tell you the truth. And so on.

When you are a CEO, you have to develop two identities: you as a person and employee of the organisation, and you as the organisation and employer. The latter must always be prioritised when it comes to organisational decisions. That is the only way to balance the proverb: power tends to corrupt, and absolute power corrupts absolutely. This will be put to the test with every decision you make about the working environment, pay, division of tasks, etc. You can use your personal experiences to give you an insight into what may benefit employees, but you must ultimately make decisions as if you would not be personally impacted by the outcome. If this is not something you can trust yourself to do, it is probably best not to become a CEO of an organisation larger than just you.

So when considering whether you want to be a CEO, ask yourself:
1. Can I embody this organisation? Can I live by the values, culture, behaviours, and work of the organisation so that I can

role model them for the rest of the team? Will this create cognitive dissonance or a moral quandary for me?

2. Do I care enough about this organisation and its work to put up with the downsides of being a CEO?
3. Can I provide stability, when everything external and/or internal is in chaos?
4. Do I find it motivating to come up with a plan and then support other people to carry it out, rather than do the work myself?
5. Do I like people? Am I able to talk to a wide range of people, in a wide range of emotional states? Can I handle difficult conversations?

The questions are in order of importance. You absolutely need to be able to say yes to the first two before you take on a CEO opportunity. If you cannot, walk away. Whatever perks that are on offer are definitely not worth it, you will not last. The third question can be mitigated with training and coaching. The fourth question may depend on the size of the organisation; if it is small enough, you will definitely need to do some of the work. The fifth question may depend on your management structures. It is also the one that training can help you find ways around, even if it does not come naturally to you.

What skills do you need as a CEO?

As the saying goes: 'what got you here, won't get you there." (Goldsmith, 2008) The skills you have exhibited that got you to the point of becoming a CEO are not necessarily the skills you will need moving forward. If you are at a very small organisation, you may still be involved in some of the day-to-day product/service delivery. But as CEO, you will now be responsible for a whole swathe of other things completely separate from your previous role. And you will need a whole new toolbox of skills to survive and thrive.

The Leadership Pipeline model (Drotter et al., 2011) outlines the different levels of leadership and the skills, focus, and values you will need at each level. While this has been developed for large organisations, it is relevant for small organisation CEOs as you will need to develop and hone the skills associated with Levels 2-5. Levels 6-7 most likely will not exist within a small organisation - these levels tend to only apply to huge multinational corporations.

However, the skills of Levels 6-7 should also be incorporated into the CEO role in their absence.

1. Self Manager - you are responsible only for yourself and the work that you do. You will need skills specific to your specialism within the organisation, focus on doing the day-to-day product/service delivery, and values linked to self-motivation and specialism expertise.

2. People Manager - this is the first level where a leader is responsible for others. You will need skills in planning; delegation; performance management; feedback and development; motivation; reporting; and recruitment. Your time should be focused on planning and setting priorities; supporting your team members; and managing the team. Your values should be linked to managerial work; delivering through others; developing others; and spending time with your team. From this level on, you need to let go of day-to-day product / service delivery and focus on being a multiplier for your teams. You need to value the success of others and trust in others to deliver.

3. Manager Leader - at this level, a leader is responsible for other managers. You will need skills in holding managers to account; coaching the managers that sit below you; setting strategy and direction; managing change; communicating with those below you; and creating a conducive work environment. Your time should be focused on assigning leadership work; monitoring progress; coaching and developing those underneath you; and coordinating with other managers. Your values should be linked to managing not doing; coaching; contributing to the organisation; and prioritising clear communications.

4. Function Leader - at this level, a leader is responsible for managing a whole function / department of the organisation such as Communications, Operations, Service Delivery. You would manage the Manager Leaders across the department. Your skills need to be in translating organisational strategy into your function's strategy; creating a positive work culture within your function; managing ambiguity and complexity; leading change; coordinating with other functions; building reputation and authority; managing people without having personal expertise in their roles. You need to focus your time

on participating in cross-function meetings; focusing on long term strategy; researching new developments in your sector; listening to direct reports; developing direct reports. You need to value working outside of your own expertise; strategic focus; learning about new things; maturity as a leader.

5. Business Leader - at this level, a leader is responsible for the whole organisation. You will have a senior leadership team underneath you made up of Function Leaders. Your skills need to be in thinking strategically across the organisation; integrating functions; long term thinking; working with a wide variety of people; managing functional differences and clashes; balancing future goals with present needs; managing financial performance and risk; and optimising performance. Your time should be focused on thinking, reflecting, and analysing; developing direct reports; defining strategy; managing external stakeholders; cultivating income; and learning about the organisational functions. You need to value trust; feedback from functions; diversity; and strategy.

6. Group Leader - at this level, a leader is responsible for several organisations. While this level of leadership is unlikely to exist within a small organisation, the skills are still relevant to a small organisation CEO. These skills include the ability to evaluate strategy; assess core capabilities of an organisation(s); understand the organisational context; allocate limited resources; and strategic differentiation. Time should be focused on resource allocation; considering growth prospects and context implications; and developing direct reports. You need to value succeeding indirectly through other people (and organisations); and strategic skills.

7. Enterprise Leader - at this level, a leader is responsible for a portfolio of organisations and areas. As with the previous level, this leadership level is unlikely to exist within a small organisation. However, the skills continue to be relevant to a small organisation CEO. Skills need to be in long term visionary thinking; ability to drive towards strategic milestones; assembling high performance teams; balancing short term with long term; seeing the larger picture; and being decisive. Your time should be focused on inspiring the entire employee team; developing direct reports; developing the organisation's external network and reputation. You need to

value trade-offs between strategic and visionary thinking; outward looking perspective; developing new things; taking advice from the Board; and asking questions and listening to a broad spectrum of people.

To summarise, as a small organisation CEO, you need to become comfortable with not doing and instead managing. Your ego will likely protest as the direct impact of your work and your role will be less obvious. You need to focus more of your time on developing those below you, supporting them to grow and be better. You will spend more time in meetings than ever before. You should not resent meetings and wish you were doing "real work" - the meetings are critical aspects of your role. You need to be intentional with these meetings, so they have clear goals and actionable outcomes. You need to be able to deal with ambiguity, gathering information both within and outside of your organisation to inform your decision making, and you need to balance the short term needs with long term plans. You need to make decisions, learn from them, and make new decisions. You need to communicate your vision for the future in a way that inspires action from the people that sit below you in the organisation and sit external to the organisation.

Who are you as a CEO?

As you balance your two identities as a person/employee and as the organisation/employer, you will need to balance your personality at work. You need to recognise that you already have different personas that you use in different situations. You may be a partner, a friend, a child, a sibling, a parent, a volunteer, an employee, etc. In the Venn diagram of your personality, there will be much overlap between these personas around the core of who you are, but there will be differences between them. You may be more reserved around your parents, more intimate with your partner, more gossipy with your friends, and more serious at work. This does not mean you are inauthentic, it means that you socially adapt to each situation you are in. It is a key part of social cohesion that people adjust around each other. As you move into a CEO role, you need to cultivate your CEO persona.

You need to balance being authentic and true to yourself while maintaining professionalism to engender credibility and trustworthiness. Goffee and Jones outline the recipe for being an "authentic leader": you need to know yourself and behave in self-consistent ways; you need to understand the context in which you are operating and adapt how you present yourself to conform enough to make people feel accepting; you need to manage your 'social distance', shifting from distance to closeness depending on the situation. This means you "will have to present different faces to different audiences." (Goffee and Jones, 2005) You need to be selective with what you disclose about you as a person and what you keep to yourself, to cultivate the image your team needs of you as the organisation. There is no rigid, single way to 'be' as a CEO. You can and should bring your true personality to it, and shine as yourself. But possibly a more polished version of yourself, someone others feel they can rely on to make decisions and keep the organisation going. As time goes on and the image of you as the organisation becomes stable and accepted, then you can reveal more of you as a person. As always, as a CEO, the organisation has to come first.

It is important to note that polished does not equate to perfect. Presenting an infallible perfect persona will only create pressure and stress on you, causing you to hide from mistakes and avoiding risks as it may reveal a less than perfect reality. A 'perfect' leader also can be very intimidating for your team, who will become distant as they feel unable to live up to the ideal and they will avoid coming to you for help as they will feel it is a sign of weakness. Combined, this will ultimately damage your organisation as mistakes will be seen as unacceptable failures, rather than as learning opportunities. As CEO, you are the role model for the organisation's behaviours. Be the employee you want to see.

What kind of CEO are you?

How you approach being a CEO will have a deep and long lasting impact on your team. You need to explore your emotional and social intelligence competencies to identify your strengths and areas for improvement, so that you can bring out the best in your people and act as a true multiplier for your team. You will need to self-reflect to identify your inner values and how you intend to be an authentic leader, so you can intentionally build trust and portray self-consistency from the moment you take on a leadership role. A leadership coach can be invaluable in helping you explore all of the above.

Once you have done this internal reflection, you can channel it into finding your leadership style. Golema (2000) identified six styles of leaders:

1. Coercive leaders - "demand immediate compliance" - these leaders have clear requirements and expect everyone to follow their orders.
2. Authoritative leaders - "mobilize people toward a vision" - these leaders craft a central mission for the organisation that acts as a North Star to guide the organisation.
3. Affiliative leaders - "create emotional bonds and harmony" - these leaders prioritise relationships with their teams and aim to keep their team happy.
4. Democratic leaders - "build consensus through participation" - these leaders involve their teams in decision making and give each employee an equal voice.
5. Pacesetting leaders - "expect excellence and self-direction" - these leaders set challenging goals and excel from the front. They expect everyone to keep up with them and continually strive for more and better.
6. Coaching leaders - "develop people for the future" - these leaders focus on building their team's skills so that they can improve over time.

While you will naturally favour one of the above leadership styles, it is important to develop your skills in several. In his analysis, Goleman has found that the most effective leaders are those who have mastered at least the authoritative, democratic, affiliative, and coaching styles; and can switch between the styles depending on their team's needs. The effectiveness of your leadership style will depend on the circumstances in which they are deployed. Developing your emotional intelligence (Goleman, 2000) and social intelligence (Goleman and Boyatzis, 2008) will help you navigate the different needs of your team. For example, in times of crisis, coercive leadership that offers calm and clear direction may be more appropriate than democratic leadership which may lead to delays and endless committee meetings. Conversely, when at a real loss in a crisis, democratic crisis management meetings that involve all voices may lead to innovative thinking and solutions.

You must also recognise that your leadership style will impact and influence the leadership styles of other managers and leaders within the organisation. As CEO, you set the tone for what is expected.

Warning

As mentioned above, you need to be aware that as CEO, team members (and the general public) will struggle to see you as separate from your title and from the organisation. Therefore, there are several things you need to be conscious of in how you present yourself, speak, and behave:

- You are the role model for behaviour in the organisation. If you believe yourself to be above the rules, then you are signalling that the rules are not important. You will create a double standard that other team members will resent. Other senior team members will start to think that power equals less (or no) restrictions and will start to interpret that in ways that suit them.
- There is always a power imbalance in your interactions with other team members. Therefore, your behaviour, your comments, and even your jokes will have more of an impact than that of another team member. Your teasing will sting more, as team members may wonder if it is informal feedback about their performance. You sharing positive news, such as booking an amazing holiday, may seem like bragging and lording your larger salary over lesser paid colleagues.
- The power imbalance also means that your colleagues attribute more weight to your requests, especially among more junior members of the team. A throwaway request from you may be treated as a mandate. You need to be mindful of this when asking for something, making clear what is a wellbeing request, or a directive.
- You will have team members with whom you have a closer personality match than other team members. However, if you are clearly more friendly with one team member or a small subset of team members, then others may interpret leniency

as favouritism. This may lead to internal resentment and rifts. Avoid meeting socially with team members outside of work, unless all of the team are invited. Treat all team members equitably and fairly, based on their performance and behaviour, rather than your personal feelings. No matter how much you like your colleagues, you are their employer first. You can be friendly, but you need to maintain a professional distance until after your employment ends.

- Remember that anything you say, do, or write could be used against you as evidence in a court of law. For example, jokes copied out of context can be used to paint you as willfully negligent. This is true for any employee within an organisation but is especially true of the CEO as you are also seen as an embodiment of the organisation. Always remember you are first and foremost fulfilling your paid employment contract in a professional place of work.

- As mentioned above, balance how much you reveal about yourself versus maintaining the image of being the organisation. Consider keeping your personal social media private. Be mindful of connecting with colleagues on social media - it opens the door to all previous behaviour and photos being linked to you in your current position. It may be appropriate to have a general rule that you will not connect on personal social media channels until after your employment ends, and then only if you want to keep in touch with them over the long term. Tread carefully around topics like your family life, social life, and dating life - it's best not to bring these topics up yourself and to be sensitive in responding to questions. Balance being authentic to build trust with your team, against maintaining the image people need to have of you as the reliable CEO that embodies the organisation. You do not need to, nor should you, share everything to be authentic.

- You embody the organisation for all those outside of the organisation. You are viewed as the spokesperson. Your behaviour, even outside of working hours, may be linked to the organisation. If you feel passionate about certain causes, you will need to consider whether those passions align with the organisation. If you behave recklessly, for example by speeding while driving, it may signal the organisation accepts

11

and endorses reckless behaviour. You do not get to 'clock out' to the same extent as other colleagues. The more publicly visible your role, the more scrutiny you will be under outside of work. You should maintain your work/life boundaries, but be conscious that someone could always be watching.

As a CEO, your responsibility is to create a safe and legally compliant workplace above all else. How you express yourself, build your authentic leadership persona, and build relationships with team members, must always exist within the confines of fulfilling your role as CEO, representing the organisation, and maintaining a safe workplace.

PART 1

INNER LIFE

As a CEO of a small organisation, you will have your work cut out for you in terms of remaining mentally healthy. You need to intentionally focus on your wellbeing and engage with it so that you can be more resilient. As a CEO, the pressure can mount and by taking control over your wellbeing, you protect yourself from the damaging effects that stress can have. Not only will this help you to maintain a balanced mindset, but it will also role model to your team what good self-care looks like, and your leadership will improve as a result. The most important thing: be kind to yourself. Recognise all of your positive attributes, while recognising your limits. It is okay to take breaks. It is okay to ask for help. Perfection is not the goal. You are enough.

Know yourself

The perfect CEO does not exist. You will not get it right the first time. Or the second time. You can only ever aim to do it as well as you can at the time that you do it. Then learn. And improve for future situations. And aim to be better tomorrow than you are today.

Remember the quote "the difference between good and great is not one big thing but a hundred things with 1% improvement". Adopting a continual improvement (or Dweck's "growth") mindset recognises that you can cultivate your skills and abilities through your efforts. We are not stuck in who we are, we can all change.

Effective reflection enables you to identify all of your existing strengths, your weaknesses, and the 1% improvements that you can implement. Build in periods of reflection at key milestones, such as the end of projects or following a challenging situation, to reflect on:
- How did the project/situation unfold? Identify the facts of the situation as objectively as possible. A timeline can help with this.
- What went well? In every situation, there will be at least one thing that went well and deserves recognition.
- How well do you think you managed the project/situation? Consider the things you had control over and influence over - what did you do well? What could in hindsight have been different?

- What could be improved in the future? Do not ruminate on what you feel went wrong. Identify the learnings that you can take away so it can be better in the future.
- What training could you benefit from to be better prepared in the future? Take each situation as a learning opportunity and identify the areas you think you should strengthen.
- What further support could you benefit from? No one can do everything alone. Identify where you could have asked for help and identify how you will into the future.
- How will you implement your learnings? What are the next steps from here? Commit to a clear plan of action, even if it is only one thing.

It is common to more readily identify weaknesses and areas for improvement, than picking out strengths. Questionnaires, such as the University of Pennsylvania's 'Authentic Happiness' project can be useful in further identifying strength attributes. You can then use your list of strengths in three main ways:

1. Draw on your strengths when you encounter a new experience or challenge. If you feel unsure about yourself, consider how each of your strengths could apply to the situation. For example, if you have to have a difficult conversation with a colleague, you might draw on your sense of justice to ensure both parties in the conversation achieve their goal; use your love of learning to see how you might develop your skills in handling difficult conversations; or use your objectivity to support both you and the colleague to move beyond your biased perspectives.
2. Identify strengths that could become specialisms. If you are naturally talented and/or you have invested time and energy in cultivating a strength, it could be an area you focus on more to enhance the strength. It could become a unique facet to you as a leader and as a person, which means you become the "go-to person" for that knowledge, skill, or attribute.
3. Mentor others around you to develop their knowledge, skills, or attributes. If you already excel in an area, it is a great value-add to your team to help them with their self-improvement. Especially in a small organisation, you may not have the budget to send staff on formal training programmes or offer

many fancy perks, but having a leader invest time in their team members and support their growth can be priceless.

You also need to be honest with yourself about your weaknesses. As no one is perfect, everyone will have areas in which they are strong and areas in which they are weak. You are not a failure if you have weaknesses, nor do you need to eliminate every weakness. Weaknesses can then be addressed in two ways:

1. Mitigate the weakness - knowing your weaknesses, you can build up a team around you who have the strengths you lack. This may involve recruiting volunteers, hiring staff, or paying external consultants. This recognises that we benefit from being part of a team where everyone's strengths complement each other.
2. Developing yourself - this tends to be a long-term approach as it can take time to change. You can seek out training, mentoring, coaching, and support to develop the knowledge, skills, and attributes you think you need. It can help to imagine a future version of yourself (for example, six months, one year, or three years in the future) where you no longer have the identified weakness. Then work back from that future point, identifying the steps you had taken to get to that future state. This will give you a rough roadmap to follow to get from the present to that future.

Remember, perfect is the enemy of good. Know yourself: where you are great, where you are good enough, and where you want to improve.

Manage your stress

Stress is a poison. It is a destructive, unhealthy, life-altering state. It is addictive and often confused with success. It is always stated that a little stress is beneficial, it keeps you focused and working through a challenge. The problem is when that stress builds up. When you associate achievement with the sense of stress. When you pile on more and more because stress means you are busy, and busy means you are being productive, and productive means you have purpose and meaning. It is a narrative trap that we have fallen into as a society.

Stress can overwhelm you unexpectedly. That is because healthy pressure can be beneficial and has been shown to be linked to performance (Yerkes and Dodson, 1908). But when the pressure tips into stress, then it starts to narrow down your life. You can start to focus on the stressors and try to 'tough out' the situation. That means that you start to give up on things separate from your source of stress, such as meeting up with friends because you feel too tired or you just need to finish off the project. As you cut out the things in life that are meant to provide resilience to stress (socialising, hobbies, exercise, work-life boundaries), you end up with only the source of stress and no clear way out. This is referred to as the exhaustion funnel and it ends with burn-out. It has been shown that the people most vulnerable to burnout are usually the most conscientious and whose level of self-confidence is closely dependent on their performance at work. This often describes a small organisation CEO.

Stress can destroy your mental and physical health. It has been shown to be linked to memory problems; insomnia; high blood pressure; weakened immune system; high cholesterol; inefficient kidney function; irritable bowel; diabetes; chronic muscle and joint pain; irritability; anxiety disorders; and depression. It is not something to brush off or 'tough out'.

When you notice stress building up, there are several actions you can take immediately to address it:
- Tell your 'line manager': you can feel overwhelmed and stressed, even if you are competent at your job. CEOs are

employees too. Where you have a board of directors/governors/trustees, one should be designated to serve as your line manager. If you do not have a governing body, then consider joining a peer network of other local small organisation CEOs, getting an external coach, or another trusted individual outside of your organisation to serve the line manager role. You deserve the same level of line management as any member of your team. It is important to share the impact of your work on you as an individual with someone who is in a position to help.

- Review the tasks at hand: if you are feeling overwhelmed, use that as a trigger to take a few minutes to plan out all the tasks at hand. What needs to be prioritised? How long will each task take? What can be done today and what needs to be delayed? Who needs to be informed where delays are scheduled to occur? This short break will serve as a "vigilance break", something that is highly recommended in high-stakes encounters such as surgeries, for all parties to review instructions and guard against error. (Pink, 2019)

- Be honest: maintain professionalism, but be honest that the circumstances are straining. If the team knows you are having a tough time, they will think about how they use you. People may just try to solve their own problems. They may consider how unreasonable they are being - although that may be wishful thinking. It sets a good example to the rest of the team that mental health problems are not just brushed under the rug.

- Take breaks: stress does not dissipate of its own accord. It is important to take time off to recover. Mental health is just as important as physical health. It is not a weakness to be mentally unwell. Pushing through may work in the immediate short term, for a day or even a week. But beyond that, you are doing more damage than good. Your work will suffer just as much as you, so it is not worth suffering through.

- It is okay to walk away: you are not a failure if you do. Not every environment is suitable for every person. Don't wait for your health - mental or physical - to fail you before you make a change.

Alongside immediate actions, there are also long term approaches to manage your stress levels and stay mentally healthy. These are detailed in the subsections below.

Find your stress red flags

The way you can reduce the impact of stress is by recognising its onset. You can learn your red flags signs for stress. There are four categories of symptoms that show up when someone is stressed:

1. Physical: more frequent headaches, persistent fatigue, constant minor illness (e.g. runny nose), indigestion, stomach pain, tinnitus, dizziness, internal shaking and weakness, shallow breathing.
2. Emotional: heightened anxiety, rumination, feeling more easily discouraged, feeling helpless or powerless, increased emotional outbursts, reduced sense of humour.
3. Mental: difficulty concentrating, impaired decision making ability, reduced time management, reduced creativity, excessive self-criticism, pessimism, boredom.
4. Behavioural: increased use of alcohol / drugs / tobacco / caffeine / sugar, altered sleeping patterns, workaholism / absenteeism, reduced socialising, reduced exercise, increased self-soothing activities (nail biting, scratching, hair pulling).

When you are next aware of feeling stressed, take a moment to check in with your physical, emotional, mental, and behavioural states to see what is happening. Over time, you will be able to pick out your red flags to mark the onset of stress.

Identify your stressors

Armed with your stress red flags, you can then notice what is setting off the red flags to find your stressors. Freestyle writing can also help identify your stressors. Freestyle writing is when you write down whatever comes into your mind without filtering or adding structure. When feeling stressed, you can write down all the thoughts and feelings that are storming inside of you. Stress can build up when there is too much internal and external information swirling around that you cannot process at once. Writing everything down reduces the amount you are trying to process, which can calm you down in the moment. Afterwards, you can reflect on what you have written to analyse the stressors. It can then be helpful to categorise your stressors against two criteria:

1. External vs internal: an external stressor is where someone or something outside of you is placing excessive pressure on you. An internal stressor is where you are placing excessive pressure on yourself.

2. Zone of the stressor: a stressor is within your "zone of control" where you have full capacity to make a change; within your "zone of influence" where you may not have the final say but you can influence change; or within your "zone of concern" where it exists in your environment but you have no direct or indirect control over it.

Challenge your perceptions

Our perception of an experience can make the difference between it being a stressor, performance-driving pressure, or just a neutral encounter. Especially when the source of the stress is internal. It is impossible to eliminate all sources of stress in life if our default perception is to find stress in what we do. The first step in changing your perception is to be aware of the perception. It can be helpful to ask yourself the following questions regarding your stressors:

- What about this makes me feel stressed? The categories you put the stressors into will help you dig deeper here.
- What do I worry or fear will happen if this thing went wrong? It is very common to create unconscious doomsday scenarios that drive feelings of stress.

It can then help to imagine being a third party observer, watching the situation that causes stress. In exploring these third party scenarios, you will often be able to confront the unconscious doomsday belief as they are rarely accurate to what would happen in real life. This can release its hold on you and let you view the stressor more calmly and rationally, which will lift a lot of its hold on you. The stressor may not be gone, but its impact on you should be smaller.

Eliminating stressors

How you go about reducing and eliminating your remaining stressors will depend on the zone categories you put them into.

Where stressors fall within your "zone of control", you have the most ability to improve things for yourself. Challenge the stressor by exploring:

- What is the actual intention of the activity behind the stressor?
- What alternative ways are there to achieve the intention, without causing the stressor?
- What is stopping you from adopting one of the alternative approaches?
- What steps could you take to get you closer to the alternative approach?

Where stressors fall into your "zone of influence", you may not be able to directly impact the stressor, but you will have the ability to influence change around you for the better. Consider:

- Who has control over the stressor, who you may need to recruit as a collaborator?
- What behaviour change is required among others to bring about the result you want?
- What is the benefit for them in making that behaviour change? Wherever possible, find a win-win. It is not a sustainable approach to bring about a benefit for yourself at the expense of a colleague. As the CEO, ultimately, you need to maintain the stress balance across the entire team, so reducing your stress levels by raising that of a direct report will just result in you then needing to support a stressed-out colleague.

Where stressors fall into your "zone of concern", you need to recognise that you will have a very limited ability to make a change. These may be ones you need to consider your perception, instead of directly trying to reduce or eliminate the source of the stressor. One of the main ways you can bring about a change in your "zone of concern" is to remove yourself from the situation.

Build your resilience

Resilience is an oft-misunderstood concept. It is not the ability to face down stress, to push through, to tough out. That is the ultimate road to burnout. Resilience is the capacity to recover quickly after a challenge, to return to your usual state after exposure to a stressor. It is something that can be cultivated and built over time. Building your resilience should sit alongside your stress management techniques - you should not expose yourself to unnecessary stress just because you can be resilient and recover.

Resilience can often be anchored around four pillars in our lives: sleep (more on this below); good nutrition; exercise (both physical and mental); and meaningful relationships. Sleep gives you energy, to think clearly, it helps you embed learning, and it helps combat a lot of serious physical and mental illnesses. Good nutrition builds on this and provides you with a potentially enjoyable experience every mealtime. Physical and mental exercise gives you space to step away from your stressors and become absorbed in a fun and stimulating activity. Meaningful connections - be they with a romantic partner, friends, family, or a community group - further enrich our experiences and provide us with a support network. These can create a positive cycle of self-care that allows us to recover from the impact of stressors and refresh us moving forward.

A powerful way to build resilience is to practice mindfulness. As Myles Downey said "awareness is curative" (Downey, 2014). Being mindful means you focus on your experiences and lets you actively respond to the situation around you, rather than reacting automatically. You can be aware of things that may potentially trigger reactions with you, and give you the space to centre yourself and choose how you react. Mindfulness is not the same as meditation, it is about zoning into your zone and experiences rather than zoning out. Mindfulness can be built into little moments each day, such as waiting for the kettle to boil or the moments before you join a virtual meeting, where you mentally check in with your physical state (your body and sensations); your emotional state (the different feelings swirling inside of you); and your mental state (the thoughts and narrative going through your mind). This builds resilience by helping you notice your stress red flags early and interrupting the unhelpful thought patterns we can get stuck in.

It can also be helpful to build in reflection time into each day. Especially during stressful times, spend 5 minutes at the end of each workday to:
1. Write down what you accomplished that day
2. Plan out the activities for the following workday
3. Note five things you appreciated that day

This will "encode the day as productive" (Pink, 2019), help you feel prepared for the following day, and counterbalance any negative experiences by appreciating the small positives that surround us.

Stress is destructive. Respect it. Do not use stress as a measure of how accomplished you are. Tell the people that you are struggling. Ask for help. Pay attention to your mental health. Be mindful. Respect yourself.

Special note on sleep
One of the most important things - if not the most important thing - you can do for your mental and physical health, for your productivity, and for the success of your organisation is to get a good night's sleep every night of the week. As Matthew Walker wrote in *Why We Sleep*: "It is difficult to imagine any other state - natural or medically manipulated - that affords a more powerful redressing of physical and mental health at every level of analysis."

Some key sleep facts to remember, all taken from Walker's book:
- Humans can never "sleep back" to make up for previously missed sleep. It is important to prioritise a good night's sleep every evening.
- Non-rapid eye movement sleep (NREM) sleep helps transfer newly learned information into long-term memory. Rapid eye movement (REM) sleep helps these new memories integrate into your existing knowledge. Therefore, disturbed sleep will disrupt your ability to learn and make new connections.
- If your sleep is chronically disrupted, you will develop physical and mental ailments, reduced alertness, and impaired memory. Chronic poor sleep is linked to Alzheimer's disease,

heart attacks, stroke, diabetes, chronic stress, gastrointestinal problems, cancer, lying, high risk behaviour, and cheating. You will deteriorate over extended periods of chronic poor sleep and may not be able to recover fully.

- "After sixteen hours of being aware, the brain begins to fail. Humans need more than seven hours of sleep each night to maintain cognitive performance."

Therefore, prioritise your sleep and have good sleep hygiene. The following will help you sleep better:

- Leave yourself enough time to get 8-9 hours of sleep, with a buffer in case it takes a while to fall asleep.
- Have a nightly routine. Eat dinner at least two hours before you go to sleep. Shower and brush teeth within an hour of going to bed.
- Do not use your phone within 30 minutes of going to bed. The advice is one to two hours before bed, but that can seem impossible at the outset and it is worth trying smaller time increments to build up the habit.
- Only use your bedroom for sleep and consensual adult fun times.
- Block out light and noise, and keep your bedroom at a comfortable temperature.
- Have a small, warm coloured light to help guide you to bed when it is time to go to sleep. Avoid using the main light.
- Take 10-15 minutes to decompress before attempting to go to sleep. Focus on positive things, such as counting 5 positive things that occurred that day.

Do not pressure yourself. If you sleep well, excellent. If you do not sleep well, you have given yourself enough time to still get sufficient sleep even if it is disturbed.

If you are finding it difficult to turn off your mind, it can be helpful to put a hand on your stomach and focus your attention on how your breathing is moving your hand. If you notice your mind drifting onto other matters, gently take note of where your mind went without any judgement and return to focusing on your breath and the movement of your hand. Once your thoughts stop being your main focus, your body will close the mental shop and you will fall asleep.

Look after yourself

Set boundaries

CEOs frequently describe their organisation as their 'baby'. Something that requires constant attention and care. It can feel like you have created something precious. You will likely have spent a lot of time thinking about its future, stayed up late worrying about it, sacrificed so that it can have the best opportunities and be its best self. Being a CEO can consume your life - especially in a small organisation where you are pressed for time and resources. It can be tempting to just do a bit more, work a bit later into the evening, check your emails on holiday, and then you realise you cannot shut it off.

It is important to set boundaries from the outset to avoid your work becoming your life. Hopefully, you get a lot of fulfilment and meaning from your work, but life should exist outside of work as well. If you already feel too deep into work = life, you can still impose boundaries and find a balance that is right for you. The following can help establish those boundaries.

Define your physical boundaries: have set spaces designated as your work space(s) and your life space(s). If you work in a physical office, this is fairly straightforward. If you work from home, this can be more difficult to achieve, especially if you are limited on space. However, it can be achieved even then. If your spaces overlap, have specific set ups that are used for work and for life. If you work from your kitchen table, then have a specific layout of your digital device and associated accessories (e.g. notebook, water bottle, etc) that you take out at the start of work time and then put away at the end of work time. Do not extend that work space from its designated area. Do not work from the sofa because you feel lazy that day. Keep it to the kitchen table. It will help you mentally compartmentalise work and help you step away out of your working hours.

Segregate your devices: it can feel very convenient to have your work emails and work systems on your personal device(s). You can quickly check on an email while it is in your mind mid-dinner or while you are on the toilet. But this turns your mind onto work and off of your life. If you and your organisation can afford separate devices, then invest in them. Only use your personal device(s) for life; only use your work device(s) for work. If you cannot afford separate devices, then create separate user accounts on the same device - one for work and one for personal use. Set up different login details, different backgrounds, different email addresses, everything you can to differentiate them. This will help build your self-discipline to not look at the other device during your work time and personal time.

Define your working hours: in a world of flexi-time this can seem very old-fashioned. But even if your working hours are not 9am to 5pm but an amalgamation of hours here and there throughout the day, give it structure. And stick to that structure. Turn on your device at the set time and then turn off your device at the set time. Do not say to yourself "oh, I'll just do 5 more minutes" or "I'll just finish this thing off". Turn it off. Especially if you are trying to break the habit of overworking. You have to be disciplined with yourself or you will not give yourself the opportunity to develop new habits. Other techniques in the sections further on in the field guide (such as setting goals, giving time to plan, creating a strategy) will help you understand your workload and plan it around your set hours. By developing your planning skills, you will become better at scheduling, managing expectations (both yours and others) about what is feasible, and getting things done in the time available.

Only when you have the habit and self-discipline to not slip straight into over-working, can you then consider flexing the boundaries. This should be done infrequently, and still within a structure. For example, in a particularly busy time, it may help your mental health to stay a little late to finish something off. If so, keep your overtime structured, usually 30 minutes to an hour after your usual end time. If the work cannot be finished by that time, then it cannot be finished that day. This can seem arbitrary, but everyone has limits on their ability to function at high capacity. Pushing ahead trying to solve an issue when you are tired will just lead to poor quality work. You will take much longer to produce the same output when tired and overworking will damage your mental health over time.

Protect your breaks: this applies to small breaks like your daily lunch break to weekends to holidays. Breaks are important to allow your body to rest and recover. If you do not take breaks, you will reduce your creative capacity over time, which again will lead to poorer quality outcomes that take longer to achieve, and poorer mental health.

Additionally, not taking breaks leads to poorer outcomes for your organisation. If you do not take breaks, you are setting up the organisation to fail. You will prevent resilience mechanisms from developing that allow the organisation to operate in your absence. You will overlook opportunities to develop your team members, preventing them from learning how to lead.

If you are someone who never takes breaks, then you will need to build up the habit slowly. As mentioned above, the organisation may well fall apart in your absence at first as you will have created a detrimental dependency. Start by taking your lunch break. Tell everyone you are turning off your work device(s) for 30 minutes so you can eat in peace. They can always contact you on your personal device(s) if there is truly an emergency. But try out for just 30 minutes.

When things do not fall apart, both you and your team will learn to feel comfortable with the difference. Incrementally increase the time - take a half day off of work. Take a day. Take the full weekend. Try a longer holiday. It may be that you absolutely need to check your emails - if so, designate a specific time when you will look and only look during that time. After a while, you will realise that you have developed your team to the point that you can take a full week out and not look at your emails once. This does not mean that you are not needed. It just means that the cogs can keep turning. This is part of your risk management - if the organisation fell apart without you, what would happen if you were absent for a reason beyond your control?

A final recommendation for setting boundaries is to put effort into developing your interests and life outside of work. Developing friendships and hobbies will make life more enticing and will help pull you away from your work during your personal time.

Set goals

Having a list of goals with achievable deadlines can be deeply motivating. Use this knowledge! If there are things you want to do but you feel unmotivated to do them, write them down. Set a timeframe by the end of which everything on the list needs to be crossed off. Put the list and a pen in a location that you regularly visit, so it cannot become hidden and forgotten about. Tell people about your list and ask them to check in on your progress. Things will get done, items will be crossed off, and you will feel like a star. Remember the great quote from Ralph Waldo Emerson: "Nothing great was ever achieved without enthusiasm."

Lists of SMART (specific, measurable, achievable, relevant, and time-based) goals are an excellent way for you to develop new habits. Humans are creatures of habit that take the easiest and laziest road whenever possible. Having clear rules for yourself as defined by your list of goals, will get you away from your main procrastination outlet and actively engaged in what you want to do. State that you will work out every other day, you will read a book a month, you will write 1000 words of your field guide every week and you will make it happen. A broad goal, like play your ukulele, does not work. A specific goal that you will practise one song on your ukulele once a week will work.

Create plans

Psychologists have proven that people have a finite capacity for decision making. This is why leaders can spend all day in meetings making decisions, only to pop into the shops on the way home and break down crying because they cannot decide what to have for dinner. "Every decision you make, little or big, diminishes a limited amount of your brain power." (Allen, 2015) Therefore, it is critical to your ability to be a leader (and balanced person who can survive outside of work) to have effective tools and techniques that can simplify your decision making.

A good way to reduce decision fatigue is to reduce the amount of load on your brain by planning ahead. On a bimonthly basis (or more frequently during a busy period), set two hours aside to review all of your projects, commitments, and responsibilities. Note down on a piece of paper everything you need / want to accomplish over the coming two months. It helps to categorise into major areas e.g. finance, governance, team management. Break down these tasks into their component parts.

Next, sketch out the coming two months of working days on a sheet of paper. Block off any meetings you have scheduled to give a real sense of the time available. Then schedule in all of the tasks, in order of priority and the sequential order in which tasks need to be completed. Once recorded manually, load all of your tasks onto an online task list so each day, the tasks of the day will appear on your list. In scheduling daily tasks, Daniel Pink's advice is to consider the timing of tasks. According to Pink, we each have a "chronotype", a personal pattern of circadian rhythms that influences our physiology and psychology. (Pink, 2019) For approximately 80% of people, peak analytic and logical thinking tends to occur during the early morning with a peak at noon; with peak insight and creative thinking occurring over the afternoon; with a smaller analytic peak in early afternoon. So think about report writing in the morning and brainstorming in the afternoon.

All of this will help in three ways. Firstly, it will remove the pressure on your active memory of trying to make sure you do not forget everything that needs to be done. You can refer to your plan at any time to refresh your memory. Secondly, it will reduce your anxiety about how you will manage to fit in all the work you have to do. You can see from your plan how each element will be addressed and that the workload is manageable. If you find you cannot fit the work into the time available, then you can manage your expectations and that of your team. You will need to evaluate the importance of each task to identify what can be deprioritised. You can also review what skills are needed for the tasks to identify what could be delegated to another team member. Thirdly, if unexpected work arises, you can visually see how it will impact the rest of your work and whether you need to reschedule, reprioritise, and/or delay other work. Things will be less likely to get forgotten.

Like with establishing work-life boundaries, it takes time and practice to develop a planning habit. Going from no planning to have a comprehensive two month plan (or longer) can be intimidating at the outset. A good place to start is to take 5-10 minutes at the start of each day to note down the tasks and goals for that day. Then spend 1-2 minutes prioritising what must be completed that day; what would be nice but is not mission-critical; what can wait until tomorrow; what could be delegated. Once daily planning feels comfortable and manageable, incrementally increase the period for which you are planning - next two days; the week; a fortnight; the month; two months. Go at a pace that feels right for you, it is better to take it slower and for the habit to become sustainable, than to rush into it and give up after a few days or weeks because it felt like too much.

Quiet the inner critic

As a small organisation CEO, you may be plagued by self-doubt and an overly critical internal voice. It can feel impossible to do a good job with limited resources and time. It can feel like you are just bumbling through, waiting for someone to realise that you do not have the knowledge or experience to be the CEO. This can also be referred to as imposter syndrome. The inner critic can wear you down to the point of giving up and running away. But the inner critic is wrong. You would not be in the position you are in if others did not believe in you and you had not demonstrated that you are capable.

So how do you overcome the inner critic? You need to balance it with your inner cheerleader. When you notice the inner critic being loud, it can be a helpful exercise to imagine presenting the critical comment before a judge. Take on the role of the inner critic ("the prosecution") and explain to the judge why the critical comment is valid. Talk about yourself in the third person, to give yourself some objective distance from the comment being made. As in a courtroom, then have your inner cheerleader argue the opposite side ("the defence"), explaining all the reasons why the critical comment is unvalid. Have the judge weigh up the evidence that supports and disputes each critical comment. The reality of the situation will always be much more positive than your inner critic initially lets you believe. Putting energy into your inner cheerleader will reduce the energy available for your inner critic. Over time, you will find that your inner monologue shifts from overly critical to a balanced consideration.

You do not want to completely eliminate your inner critic. It serves a useful function to prevent arrogance and thoughtless decision making. It can help you more fully think through decisions, to pick the best possible option based on the available decision. Just make sure you have enough ammunition for your inner cheerleader when the inner critic gets too loud. Julie Zhuo recommends creating a 'Little Wins' journal, in which you can note down anything you have done that you are proud of, even if it is a very small accomplishment.

Get support

As previously mentioned, you deserve the same level of line management as any member of your team. In a small organisation, this can be challenging to achieve and you will need to designate someone to serve as your line manager. This could be a member of the board of directors / governors / trustees, it could be an external consultant / mentor / coach. Your line manager's role is to enable you to be the best version that you can be at work. Follow Julie Zhuo's advice: "The key is to treat your manager as a coach, not as a judge...Engage your manager for feedback...see 1:1s with [your] manager as an opportunity for focused learning." (Zhuo, 2019)

Set up regular one-to-one meetings at least once a month to discuss your key priorities and how you are managing work. Prepare for these meetings by thinking through the following:
- Key developments since your previous meeting - what are their thoughts on your progress? How are they evaluating your success?
- Priorities moving forward - do they agree with how you have prioritised your work? Do they see additional or other priorities you should be considering?
- Challenges and/or barriers you are facing - how do you propose addressing these? Any advice from your line manager?
- Your mindset and feeling at work - what additional support could be put in place to help you?
- Personal development opportunities

For your personal development, talk through with your line manager what they see as opportunities to build on your strengths and your areas for improvement. It may be useful to consider together what a hypothetically perfect person in your role would look like, and what training you might need to get closer to that ideal.

Embrace training opportunities that the organisation is willing to support you with, both informal and formal. Your line manager will have a wealth of experience that you can pick their brains on. Whenever you have a situation where you feel unsure or inexperienced, make a note, and talk it through with your line manager at your next one-to-one. When you consider formal training, a good rule of thumb is to ask the question "one year from now, will I be happy I did this?" (Zhuo, 2019). If yes, then sign up!

As always, reflect on your progress. At least on a six monthly basis, reflect on the areas where you have improved and identify the areas you want to improve during the next six months. This will help you feel positive about progress and also set goals to keep you motivated.

Give yourself permission to feel

Feeling your emotions enriches your life. The ideal state is not a neutral, stable robot that does not feel. That road only leads to self-denial and self-suppression, which can cause damage to your relationships, mental health, and physical health. You can feel and still be stable. Still see objectively. Emotions do not equal chaos. A healthy relationship with emotions can help you learn more fully, engage with others, and lead a content life.

The RULER technique, as developed by Marc Brackett (2019), allows you to develop emotional stability. It also allows you to help others manage their emotions, and builds the foundations for emotional intelligence. RULER stands for:
- Recognise - recognise that you are experiencing an emotion. Check in with your body to identify that something is influencing your mental and physical state.
- Understand - understand what caused the emotional state to arise. Reflect on what you were thinking about, what interaction you just had, what you just smelled / tasted / heard / touched / saw? Brackett explains that there are two kinds of

emotions: integral (directly caused by the action at hand) and incidental (infiltrate our thinking without us being aware). Emotions are data - by paying attention to them, you can understand what is going on within you.

- Label - add a label to the emotion you are feeling. The Feelings Wheel is an excellent resource to help narrow in on the correct label. It'll likely be that you are feeling a mixture of emotions, all with their own causes that you can then start to analyse. As the saying goes, 'if you can name it, you can tame it', giving the emotion a name makes it feel tangible and gives you power to do something with it.
- Express - decide how and with whom you would like to express your emotional state. Reduce the emotional labour of hiding emotional states by finding appropriate ways to express yourself.
- Regulate - stabilise your emotional state so that you are in control of yourself and how you behave. Brackett recommends the following five methods:
  o Mindful breathing - taking a pause and focusing in on your breathing can allow you to calm, clear your mind, and identify how you want to proceed. This is very helpful in the moment if there is a strong overwhelming sense of an emotion.
  o Forward-looking strategies - when there is something that regularly triggers an emotional reaction, during times of calm, you can think ahead to triggering situations and identify how you may react to alter the emotional impact.
  o Attention-shifting strategies - when an emotional response is too overwhelming, a short-term response can be to distract yourself or distance yourself from the trigger, so you can calm down. If in an interaction with someone else, it is useful to use the term 'emotional hijacking' to state that an emotion has overwhelmed you and you need to step away before you can proceed with the interaction. While distancing, try to do an activity that balances your emotional state. For example, if the emotional state is high energy (e.g. excitement, anger) then find something that is calming like listening to soft music.

Conversely, if you are feeling very low (e.g. disenchanted, depressed) then find something that is more high energy like watching comedy or doing exercise.

- o Cognitive reframing - consciously choose to view the situation in a way that reduces the emotional impact. It can help to imagine standing in front of a judge and having to present both the prosecution and the defense. E.g. That person is deliberately trying to upset me vs. that person is trying to achieve their own goal and has not realised that their approach is upsetting me. Cognitive reframing especially helps with happiness. Remember the central formula: Happiness equals reality minus expectations.
- o "Meta-moment" - combining the above, when triggered, take a moment to pause, breathe, consider how your best self would respond to the situation, breathe, and then act. It can help to talk to yourself in the third person: to think about what you would advise someone else to do in the situation, give yourself space and clarity on the situation, and trigger empathy for yourself.

As mentioned above, the RULER technique allows you to develop your emotional intelligence. According to Goleman (2008), there are five facets of emotional intelligence:

1. Self-awareness - this is met by Recognise, Understand, Label
2. Self-regulation - this is met by Express and Regulate
3. Motivation - drive to achieve beyond external reward.
4. Empathy - ability to understand the emotional state of others. By practising the RULER technique, you can better recognise, understand, and label the emotions of others around you. Self-awareness also allows you to avoid 'attribution bias', where you incorrectly interpret someone's cues and behaviours by projecting your own emotional state.
5. Social skill - managing relationships, building networks, developing rapport. Your self-awareness and self-regulation make this possible as the interactions can be more meaningful and productive without emotional hijackings.

Building your emotional intelligence will enable you to be a better leader at work, build stronger relationships, and ultimately be more content in yourself and your life.

A note on being good enough

Running a small organisation, there can be significant internal and external pressure on you to grow the organisation; reach more people; be more influential. This focus on more can trap us in a destructive addiction: where we strive for more, only for the sake of having more. There is no reason behind the aim: it is not more as a means to an end, it is more as an end to itself.

This is dangerous as there can be no achievement of a goal if there is no goal to begin with. If you just want more, then when you get more, you will want more than that. And that then makes it difficult to be content with what you have. That makes it difficult to step away from work, ending in a negative spiral of working more, building more, wanting more. Like all addictions, this can lead to risky and damaging behaviours chasing the bigger dopamine release.

The way to break the addiction for more is to set goals in relation to yourself and/or your organisation, against the measures you believe are important. This should be driven by your personal and/or organisation's purpose and values. This can be influenced by external factors, for example, your funders or investors have defined criteria for what 'good' looks like. But it has to be defined, so you know when you have achieved it.

By defining the goal, you can personally release the stress of striving for a moving target. You can still strive, but it will be towards a purpose and a defined achievement point. You will know when you have done enough and you will be able to be satisfied and content in achieving it.

Where the goal is an organisational one, you can then rally your team and external stakeholders around achieving the goal. You can explain the 'why' behind it and then people can use their own creativity to suggest ways to achieve it. You give yourself permission to say no to certain opportunities, as they would take you away from the goal. Having a goal lets you set timelines around its achievement, managing everyone's expectations. It helps you recognise and appreciate progress. On a day to day basis, it can then help you recognise you have done your best in progressing towards the goal and then step away from work for the day. This is ultimately the first step towards creating an organisational strategy, which is explored fully in Part 2: Strategy.

A note on being a young CEO

Being a young CEO brings its own set of challenges, which likely overlap with and intersect with challenges faced by someone in any minority category. 'Young' is context-specific, defined generally as below the average age of CEOs in your particular culture. A quick internet search suggests that the average age of CEOs in the UK is approximately 55 years old. The further you get away from that average, the more likely you will experience the below described challenges. The positive news upfront: you will eventually age out of these challenges!

So what are the challenges you may face?

Firstly, you will likely be inexperienced. Not just at being a CEO, but in general. The younger you are, the more likely that your team members will have more experience in the working world than you. This may cause you to doubt yourself and undermine your own authority, or conversely, cause you to be brash and arrogant as you compensate for your lack of knowledge. It can also cause your team to doubt your ability, second-guess decisions, or try to dominate you through an incorrect belief that age equates to knowledge.

What you need to recognise is that you are in your role for a reason. If you set up your organisation, then you know it better than anyone else and you were able to create something out of nothing. If you were hired into your role, then a panel of people who did not know you deemed you worthy of the position. So trust in your worthiness to hold the position - but do not let this go to your head. Acknowledge and accept that you still have much to learn. Embrace the opportunity to learn. Recognise the value of experience and listen to people's suggestions. This does not mean you have to agree with them or act on their suggestions, but be open to listening and understanding. Seek out people you respect and ask them for advice. Absorb information and then make your decision to the best of your ability. That is all you can do. You will definitely look back a few years later and recognise that you could have done things better. Do not be discouraged by this. The fact that you will know better means that you have learned and grown.

With regards to your team, you should not shy away from your age. Acknowledge it but then move on. Do not let it define you. Let your performance as a CEO define you. Again, you need to own the knowledge that you are worthy of your position. If you project this confidence, the team will fall in line. When you take on the role, they will find ways to subtly (or not subtly) challenge you. It can feel like they are only doing this because you are young, but they will do this to any new leader. You will need to stand firm and stand up for yourself if you feel you are being unduly pressured or manipulated. Treating your team with respect, setting agendas, making decisions, and following through on commitments will establish you as a leader, same as anyone else. There may be the odd joke or reference to your age, but generally people will move on. After a few months, they do forget about it and can be genuinely shocked when someone else mentions it.

The second challenge you will face is the external reaction to your age. When you walk into a meeting, others may think you are the intern and overlook you. When meeting with other CEOs, they may speak over you, repeat the point you just made, and get credit for your point. External partners may prefer to deal with an older member of your team. You'll notice raised eyebrows, nervous laughter, or pure judgement when you introduce yourself as the CEO.

Part of dealing with this challenge is just to accept that this will happen. There are ways to minimise it, but until you age out of the 'young' category, it will happen. If you expect it, then the impact of the looks and reactions on your self-esteem and self-belief will lessen. We all make snap judgments based on first impressions. Your age will possibly be the first thing someone else notices about you, especially if it is a context where everyone else has a few decades on you. You are young. You can do nothing about it. They can do nothing about it. They have noticed it. Move on and they likely will too.

If you want to minimise the reaction to your age, there are several ways to deal with it. One way is to realise that the estimation of age is based on appearance. You can artificially 'age' yourself in other people's estimations through the way you present and carry yourself. Hairstyles, makeup styles, clothing styles, shoe choices, bag choices, posture all project an impression of age. Just walking into a room with a straight back and good posture projects that you have a right to be there and people generally accept it. A firm handshake, good eye contact, and good social skills imply a maturity that people assume comes with age. This does not mean that you have to give up your uniqueness so you can blend in. It means being thoughtful about how you present yourself and the impact it has on others.

Likewise, how you behave in a meeting can also project maturity. Paying attention to meetings, listening to what others are saying, all while sitting in a comfortable and engaged way (not over-eager forward on the table or making copious notes like the group secretary) imply a calm confidence. When you stand out in a group, it can feel like you are on show and need to establish your credibility by continually contributing to the conversation. This will likely put you on edge and lead to poorly worded comments that make you feel embarrassed. It can be good to give yourself a target initially to only contribute one meaningful and valuable thing to each meeting. This will mean you listen and learn. It will also mean you can take your time and only speak when it will be impactful. This will mean that the others around the table come to value you speaking and think highly of your capability. Again, this will help externals look beyond your age and see you for who you truly are.

Another approach is to build up allies for these challenging settings. People tend to be more accepting in one-to-one settings and revert to stereotypes and traditions in group settings. Finding opportunities to work one-on-one with others is a good way of building rapport, building credibility, and moving beyond initial impressions. If you are at a group meeting, find an excuse to chat one-on-one with a fellow attendee during a break. The more established and respected that person is within the group, the better. Ask for their opinion on how things are going, what they think has not yet been fully dealt with, what they think is still outstanding, what they would like to achieve, etc. Ask questions and listen to them. Where you have insights, add this to the conversation, but try to maintain a 20:80 ratio of you talking to them talking. This type of positive interaction will help that person start to see you as part of their in-group and they will start to treat you as such in the group meeting. When one or more of the group starts to treat you with respect and recognition, the rest of the group tends to follow. They will start to listen when you speak and credit you with your points. Again, with time, you will become part of the in-group due to common experiences you will go through together.

Finally, you need to recognise that no matter what you do, your age may cause an insurmountable barrier in some situations. Certain people will cling to their prejudices and always prefer to deal with one of your older team members. In these situations, you need to evaluate the value for your organisation of dealing with those people. If you cannot avoid those people, then strategise on how you will manage them. Beyond your own ego, is there a reason why you as the CEO have to be the organisational representative? There may be reasons for you to still be the person to deal with those prejudiced people. You may wish to make a statement and challenge their prejudice; use their discomfort as a negotiation advantage; or accept the situation and make the best of it while you look for alternative options. Referring back to a previous section, know yourself, your strengths, and your weaknesses. It is okay to accept that your age may be a shortcoming in certain situations and use other team members' age as a strength for the organisation.

To end on a positive note, congratulations on being a young CEO! It is a huge accomplishment. You also have several unique benefits from being a young CEO. As young CEOs tend to be less experienced in the world of work, this tends to mean you have not been overly biased by "the way things are done". You can see through ineffective and inefficient traditions, side-step entrenched beliefs, and embrace new beneficial innovations. Your age will be seen as an advantage by stagnant organisations looking to shake things up. Your existence will signal that change is to come and people will be primed for change when you are appointed. You can build a legacy early in your career and see it evolve as you grow. It is an exciting and privileged position. Well done!

PART 2

CEO-ING

Acquiring a new job

If you are setting out to become a CEO of a small organisation, remember that the more preparation you put in ahead of time, the more likely it is that you will find the right role for you. Be selective. Be prepared. It's better to take longer to find the right role, than end up in a place that is a bad fit. Find somewhere that will treat you right!

Searching

Before you start looking at vacancies, create a list of what you want out of your next role. This should include the practical elements (e.g. salary band, hours, location), the soft elements (e.g. feel like work has a positive impact on society), and your personal development goals (e.g. you want to learn how to lead an internationally based team).

It may help to create a base level SWOT analysis (Strengths, Weaknesses, Opportunities, Threats) for yourself to identify what you want to keep doing, how you want to develop, and what areas need to be improved. You may also find it useful to create a pros and cons list for your current role, so you can identify what elements you want to see in your new role and what elements you want to avoid.

With this groundwork, you will not waste time applying for jobs that you would not accept even if it was offered to you. You should therefore have more time and energy to go after the roles you really want.

As a first step, update your generic CV to fit with the type of role(s) you are interested in applying for. Make sure it captures all of the strengths you identified in your SWOT and underplays all of the identified weaknesses. It can help to show your generic CV to someone experienced whom you trust to identify gaps and potentially negative interpretations of your CV which your own blind spots can hide from you.

Applying

Most important step: only apply to jobs you actually want!

If you are very early on in your career or it has been a long time since you last changed jobs, it is often advised that you apply to a lot of jobs just to get the experience of the application / interview process. This can be beneficial, but it can also take up a lot of time and energy to get the most out of the experience. Additionally, if the role is not right for you, then you are unlikely to be right for it. This can therefore mean you spend ages applying, get your hopes up (even if you do not want the job), and then get a sense of rejection if the organisation agrees that you are not right for it / it is not right for you. If you have time, energy, and emotional stability to spare, go for it! If not, then prioritise the roles you actually want.

When you find a role you are interested in, do low-level background checks on the organisation by checking their website, annual accounts, and publicity (Google search). Check your network to see if you know anyone who used to work at / with the organisation who might be able to offer you more insight, Based on this information:
- Do their values align with yours?
- Does the organisational culture fit with your expectations?
- Does the role and organisation tick the boxes you want to be ticked?

If yes, then commit to applying.

Second most important step: make sure you follow the instructions on how to apply!

Unless instructed otherwise, adapt your generic CV to make sure that each point in the job specification and person specification is covered to the extent that you are able to demonstrate fit. Write your cover letter to address each essential and desirable point in the person specification, with relevant examples from your career. With each point, aim to follow the Point Evidence Explanation structure to outline why each example will be relevant to the role. Include at least a paragraph which outlines why you are interested in the specific role at the specific organisation. Your earlier SWOT analysis should help fill this in. Neither the CV nor the cover letter should be longer than 2 pages each - unless instructed otherwise.

Save all materials related to the job advert in a folder for later reference. These materials tend to disappear after the application deadline, which makes it difficult to prepare for the interview(s) if they are not saved on your own device.

Preparing

If you are invited to the next stage of the application process, then you will need to prepare. Read the following information about the organisation:

- Website for overview on their aims, values, activities, and 'voice' as an organisation
- Social media to review the extent to which they 'live' their values and voice
- Annual reports of activities to review impact and effectiveness (either on the website / Charity Commission / Companies House)
- Annual accounts to review financial position (either on the website / Charity Commission / Companies House)
- Regulator website to review the limits and requirements places on the organisation
- Open online search for news on the organisation
- Sector analysis to review the context in which the organisation operates and the anticipated developments that will impact them

Create a top-level PESTEL (political, economic, social, technological, environmental, legal) and SWOT (strengths, weaknesses, opportunities, threats) analysis of the organisation based on the information collected (see section on Strategy below).

From this analysis, build out a top-level 3-5 year strategy, with 3-5 main objectives you believe will need to be achieved. Review this strategy to identify the following:

1. Are you excited by this strategy? Do you think you will enjoy working at the organisation to deliver the strategy for the next 3-5 years? If your answer is no, then this organisation is unlikely to be a good fit.
2. What gaps exist in the information that you reviewed? Use these gaps to shape your questions for the interview panel.

This will both demonstrate that you have done your research and you will gather more information to help you answer the previous question.

The above exercise will also help you prepare for the interview. Most interview processes for a CEO position requires candidates to deliver a presentation and/or answer questions on their strategy for the organisation, should their application be successful.

Beyond reviewing the organisation and its suitability as your next place of employment, you will also need to prepare to demonstrate that you are suitable for the organisation. To do this, you will need to:
1. Update your SWOT analysis for your fit with the role.
2. Review each item of the job specification and list out relevant examples of your experience that demonstrate your competence in each category. Avoid repeating examples so the interviewers do not think you are milking a few cases of good practice and the rest of the time you are mediocre. While you want to make sure your examples span your career, you should include more examples from your more recent roles to demonstrate ongoing fit.
3. Review who you will be meeting with e.g. team members, interview panel members, outgoing postholder to identify commonalities to build rapport during the interview process.
4. Prepare answers for the most common interview questions:
    - Tell us about yourself.
    - Why are you interested in this post and/or in working at this organisation?
    - Why are you leaving your current role?
    - What are your key responsibilities in your current role?
    - What have been major challenges in your current role? How have you solved these challenges?
    - What is your greatest strength?
    - What is your greatest accomplishment?
    - How do you evaluate success?
    - What is your greatest weakness?
    - What areas of development and/or training needs have you identified?

- Describe a difficult situation that you had to deal with?
- What is your ideal work environment?
- What are your values and how do you live them?
- How do you manage a team?
- How do you manage team conflict?
- Describe the pace at which you work?
- How do you handle stress and/or pressure?
- What motivates you?
- What are your career goals? Where do you see yourself in 5-to-10 years?
- [Age specific - fortunately, you'll grow out of this question!] Are you ready for this position so early in your career?

Interviewing

Check the route to the interview location, identifying where you can lock up your bike/park/be dropped off by a taxi. Make a note of the time it takes to get there so you can leave without being anxious about arriving late.

Review photos of the interview panel available online - dress in a style that suits their general appearance while erring on the side of business formal. First impressions make a big impact, so it can be beneficial to mute your appearance in the interview. In general, avoid loud colours, large areas of bare skin, and dramatic make-up. This does not mean you have to hide all of your personality and become a neutral mannequin. It is a small way to subconsciously signal that you belong in the group, so they do not out-group you before they get to know you. They will only be able to draw limited conclusions and therefore will need to pay attention to what you say.

Print off your preparatory notes ahead of your interview and take them with you. Take any other items you have been instructed to bring - for example, proof of identity, certificates of qualifications.

As part of the CEO interview process, you will likely have interviews with representatives of your team (depending on the organisation size, this could be all team members); and members of the governing body. It is good to prepare questions to ask each group of interviewers, to demonstrate your engagement in the process, build rapport, and build your understanding of the role.

Questions to ask your potential new team:
- What challenges are facing them as a team? What challenges are facing the organisation?
- What opportunities do they feel are open to them? What opportunities are available for the organisation?
- How would they describe the working environment / culture at the organisation?
- How do they feel most supported at work?
- What are they expecting/hoping for in the new postholder?

Questions to ask members of the governing body:
- What do they see are the challenges and opportunities facing the organisation?
- How would they describe the working environment / culture at the organisation?
- What do they see as the priorities for the first 6 to 12 months?
- What does a successful appointment look like to them?
- Practicalities of the new role: when will they make their decision? When would they like the new postholder to ideally start? Will there be a handover period?

Accepting (or not)
When you get home, based on the information shared during your interview, update your role checklist and review the following questions:
- Do their values align with yours?
- Does the organisational culture fit with your expectations?
- Do the role and organisation tick the boxes you want to be ticked?

Be prepared for a call at the end of the day offering you the role - if they really liked you they may call earlier than the time they said in the interview that they could let you know.

If the organisation ticks your boxes, be ready to say a provisional yes to their offer.

If the organisation does not tick your boxes after the interview, withdraw your candidacy politely as early as possible. It is not fair for them to consider you and potentially reject other candidates if you do not intend to accept the role.

Where references are specified, send a polite message to your references to check they are happy to act as a reference, send them a copy of the job description, and a brief overview as to why you want the job. This will help prepare them to give an accurate and appropriate reference. Make sure to send them a thank you follow up email once they have given the reference.

Transitioning

Congratulations on your new CEO position!

It is important to recognise that changing jobs involves a defined transition period, where you learn and fit into the new role. While you will feel the pressure to prove yourself, focus mainly on information gathering and creating a strategy rather than rushing in to make decisions.

Prior to taking on the role

In preparing for your new role, you will need to be in information gathering mode. You will need to understand the following practicalities:

- When is your first day? Hours? Location?
- Will you have the equipment you need for your first day? How will you have access?

Ahead of your first day, you should also try to arrange meetings with:

- Head of the governing body
- Team
- Outgoing postholder

Head of the governing body

The aim of meeting with the head of the governing body is to build rapport and set expectations. The roles of the CEO and the head of the governing body will be closely interlinked, and a professional and functional relationship is required for your organisation's success. The first meeting should be an informal meeting, such as lunch. The following questions may be useful:

- What are their expectations for the dynamics between your role and theirs?
- What is their management style?
- What is their vision for your role?
- What do they see as the priorities for the first 6 to 12 months?
- What skills do they think a hypothetically perfect person in your role would have?
- Do they have any recommendations for things to read to build your broader contextual awareness and knowledge?

- Personal questions: what do they enjoy doing outside of work? Any hobbies? Family? Pets? Have they read / watched anything interesting recently? Travelled anywhere they would recommend?

Do not treat the meeting as an opportunity for a drive-by questioning, where you rattle through a list of questions. Aim for a natural conversation, using the above list of questions as a guide should conversation falter.

Team

The aim of meeting with your team is to build rapport and to make sure you all feel comfortable with each other on your first day. It is a good opportunity to connect as individuals, before the power dynamics become established. This should be an informal meeting, such as a coffee. The following questions may be useful:
- What do they enjoy doing outside of work? Any hobbies?
- Have they read / watched anything interesting recently?
- Have they travelled anywhere they would recommend?

Make it clear that you intend to meet with each team member one-on-one once you start in post to better understand your working dynamics, get a better sense of each role, and build your knowledge for the role. This meeting should solely be focused on getting to know each other better.

Outgoing postholder

Finally, the aim of meeting with the outgoing postholder is to gather as much information as possible to help you jump into the role. The following questions may be useful:
- What requires immediate attention?
- How would they recommend you learn about the sector quickly and efficiently?
- What training would they recommend? What training have they found useful for their role?
- How would they describe the working environment/culture at the organisation?
- What are the dynamics like in the team?
- What are the dynamics like with the governing body?

- What are key external partners/relationships that need to be built/maintained?
- What was their mission for the organisation?
- What outstanding ambitions/targets do they have for the organisation?
- What do they see are the challenges and opportunities facing the organisation?
- What do they see as the priorities for the first 6 to 12 months?
- Why are they leaving? What are they going on to do?
- What materials have they prepared for the transition?
- Will they be available in the future for questions?

Remember that the outgoing postholder's perspective on the organisation and the team will be biased by their own experiences, strengths, and weaknesses. Their views may not match your own. There may be a lot of valuable insight they share, but there may also be a lot you wish to learn for yourself and do differently.

First three months in post

The first three months in a new post are critical in getting a thorough understanding of the organisation, the team, and the work you will need to do. It is a transition period for all - for you, your team, and your stakeholders. Recognise that as you try to establish yourself in your new role, everyone around you will be looking to establish themselves in the new status quo. Give people the space and permission to change along with you.

Landscape scanning

Approach your first three months as a sponge for organisational information. You will want to read the following documents to establish your foundational knowledge:
- Strategic and operational plans
- Regulation and guidance
- Previous 3-5 years of governing body minutes
- Financial plan and budget
- Key policies and procedures
- Relationship history with the communities/clients/funders the organisation works with

If any of the above documents do not exist, make a note as this will form one of your priorities as CEO to ensure the appropriate organisational infrastructure is in place.

Alongside document review, you should prioritise meeting with the following people in a one-on-one setting within your first month:
- Team members
- Chair of the governing body
- Your assigned line manager (as an employee of the organisation, you should have a line manager assigned. This is usually a member of the governing body - often the Chair)
- Each member of the governing body
- Representatives of the communities/clients/funders the organisation works with

After your first month, also send introductory emails and ask for meetings with external stakeholders such as:
- External suppliers (e.g. HR, finance, legal)
- Key partners
- Regulators

Write detailed notes and take time at the end of each day to reflect on what you have learned, what gaps in the information do you see, what questions you have, and what further actions you need to take to gather more information.

Team members
Aim to meet with each member of your new team within your first two weeks. Set the context for the meeting that you want to get to know them, their working styles, what they would like to see continue, and how they want to see the organisation change under your leadership. This is the first step in building a trusted and respectful relationship with each member of the team. The following questions should be covered, alongside any additional specific questions you may have from your initial research:
- How long have they been at the organisation?
- What is their role? *[This can be both formal and informal, e.g. their role within the team dynamics]*
- What are their current priorities?

- What is their preferred management style? How do they like to be supported? How do they like to receive feedback? What relationship do they want to have with their manager/CEO?
- What do they expect from a CEO? What qualities do they expect a CEO to embody? *[Explore and promise to uphold the expectations you agree with]*.
- What do you as a CEO expect from them? *[Explore and ask them to in turn promise to uphold their expectations.]*
- What do they like about working at the organisation?
- What challenges do they have in their role?
- What opportunities do they see for themselves in the role?
- What challenges does the team have?
- What opportunities do they see for the team?
- What challenges do they see for the organisation?
- What opportunities do they see for the organisation?

Recognise that team members may want to reinvent themselves with a new manager. Therefore, it is worth checking previous HR records (e.g. appraisal notes, personnel folder) but do not let yourself be overly biased by their content (unless someone has an active and ongoing HR issue).

Chair/governing body members
In meeting with the governing body members, it should be a more informal meeting exploring the following questions:
- What are their expectations for the dynamics between your role and theirs?
- What is their vision for your role?
- What do they see as the priorities for the first 6 to 12 months?
- What skills do they think a hypothetically perfect person in your role would have?
- Do they have any recommendations for things to read to build your broader contextual awareness and knowledge?
- How would they describe their level of involvement in the organisation? How involved would they like to be?

Representatives of the community
In meeting with representatives of the community that your organisation works with, keep the meeting informal, respectful, and aimed at building rapport. Explain you are new in the role and have

asked to meet to build your understanding and make sure the community's voice is always heard under your leadership. You will not have any answers and you will come back to the community to outline your strategy once you have had time to settle. Explore the following questions:

- What is their lived experience?
- What has been their previous experience working with the organisation?
- What elements of the organisation do they think work well? What would they like to see continue?
- What elements of the organisation could be improved? Why? How?
- What is their vision/hope for the organisation in the future?

External stakeholders

Meetings with external stakeholders should be more formal, aimed at understanding the dynamics between them and your organisation; and areas they want to explore moving forward. The following questions may be appropriate:

- What is the intention/goal of the relationship between them and your organisation?
- How do they and your organisation work together?
- How did they work with/interact with your predecessor?
- What would they like to see continued under your leadership?
- What would they like to see changed under your leadership?
- What will be the interaction/dynamic between you and the representative you are speaking with?

Based on your continued research and meetings, build a list of what works well within the organisation and what could be improved. This will guide your strategy on what should be kept and what you will need to change. Prioritise the list based on "what will act as greatest multipliers" (Zhuo, 2019), i.e. what will have the biggest positive impact that you can enact.

Present this strategy to your team to get their feedback, agree on timelines, and assign responsibilities. Remember, it is not your job as CEO to fix everything! Assigning responsibilities to team members other than yourself will show that you listen and you respond, while avoiding a 'hero complex' that the new CEO has come to save everyone and is the only one who can improve things.

Developing team dynamics

A new CEO allows the team to evaluate their own working dynamics, behaviours, and culture in order to make changes. You will need to focus this change on building trust and a supportive culture.

As Brené Brown wrote, trust is "earned in the smallest of moments. It is earned not through heroic deeds, or even highly visible actions, but through paying attention, listening, and gestures of genuine care and connection." (Brown, 2018) To be a trusted leader, you need to put in the effort to build a connection with each of your team members; you need to check in and make sure they feel listened to and respected. It is helpful to create a document on each team member and record information they shared about themselves, such as partners' names, number of children and names, pet's names, hobbies, past working history, etc. This will serve as a memory aid for you as you grapple with the tsunami of information you have to process at the start of a new job while demonstrating to your team that you do listen and care.

It is crucial that you create a psychologically safe and supportive culture in a team. Unless people feel they can share their thoughts without fearing criticism and reprimands, the team will be hindered in their effectiveness, creativity, and innovation. In order to encourage people to be open, honest, and inquisitive in meetings, start your first team meeting by asking individuals to write down one thing they need from the others to feel safe sharing and asking questions, and one thing that will impede them from doing so. Have everyone reveal these at the same time and jointly agree to uphold those behaviours during the meeting. That way, if anyone misbehaves, it is easy to raise the issue, resolve it, and carry on without much interruption. It also may encourage the quieter team members to speak up (Brown, 2018).

Look to arrange at least one team-building outing within your first three months to allow an informal opportunity for the team's new dynamics to consolidate. There will be longer-term work on building the organisation's culture and dynamics, described in more detail in other sections. But these immediate actions taken in your first three months will help set everyone off on the right path.

Practicalities

Alongside getting a handle on the broader strategic and cultural dynamics, there are several practical things you will need to do as a new CEO:

- Read all the HR and Health and Safety policies - you will need to embody these and enforce them, so you need to know what exists.
- Get access to HR systems and understand your role in monitoring these systems.
- Get access to all bank accounts and investment portfolios - also understand who currently has access, signatory rights, and how you will need to work with them.
- Understand financial policies and procedures, specifically related to paying invoices, payroll, pensions, and annual accounting - who does what, when, how? What is your role?
- Get access to Companies House and Charities Commission (where applicable). Make a note of the deadlines for submitting Compliance Statements and Annual Accounts.
- Understand what task tracking software is currently used - if none, then set up your preferred platform to record all of your actions and add deadlines.
- Review filing systems so you know where to find what, how it is structured, and how to add information to the systems.

Strategy

There is an accepted business saying accredited to Peter Drucker, that "culture eats strategy for breakfast". I disagree. Yes, culture can destroy an organisation's ability to achieve a strategy. However, without a strategy, the culture will flounder and the organisation will drift. You cannot know if you have a good culture unless you can define what 'good' is. And you need a strategy to define what is 'good' for your organisation. Once you have a strategy, you can understand the values, behaviours, and people you will need, and then as CEO you can shape the culture to fit. Your strategy should be the starting point from which everything else in the organisation flows: everything should be set up to help achieve it and to absorb the impact of unexpected complications. Your strategy will evolve and change over time, but it should remain the central engine driving the organisation forward.

Strategic thinking pitfalls

Before starting your strategic planning, you need to recognise that no matter how logical and rational you think you are being, you are very much being led by biases, preconceptions, heuristics, and emotions. You need to be aware of the pitfalls, so you can mitigate them as much as possible.

As Einstein remarked, "Common sense is the collection of prejudices acquired by age eighteen." Instincts are based on past experiences, interactions, situations, and contexts. While these can evolve over time, we tend to only notice what matches our internal belief systems and identified context. Studies have suggested that the brain is capable of processing approximately 11 million bits of information every second, but our conscious mind can handle only 40-50 of those bits (Agarwal, 2020). Therefore, we form heuristics to make sense of all of that information, based on our 'common sense'.

This can limit your strategic thinking, as your past experiences will influence how you think ahead and feel about the future. Some key limiting heuristics are:
- The endowment effect: overvaluation of what we already have

- Status quo bias: an emotional preference for maintaining the status quo
- Loss aversion: the tendency to attribute much more weight to potential losses than potential gains when assessing risk
- Availability heuristic: the tendency to judge the likelihood of an occurrence based on the relative ability to imagine it happening
- Representativeness heuristic: more readily discern cause and effect if the effect of a given action seems logically related to the assigned cause

In addition, risk detection and risk avoidance (both key parts of strategic planning) are believed to be linked to emotional processing in the brain. As Taleb (2007) summarised, this means that "rational thinking has little, very little to do with risk avoidance."

Without sustained effort and attention, it is easy to fall into heuristic traps. It can be partially overcome through what is called 'system 2' thinking which is rational and logical, as opposed to 'system 1' unconscious reasoning (Kahneman, 2012). You can challenge your assumptions, identify information gaps, and read more widely. However, the best way to avoid the traps is to have a diverse team around you, with a wide range of experiences and backgrounds, that are confident in calling out your assumptions, biases, and preconceptions in a constructive and supportive manner. You need to find "thinking partners who aren't echo chambers", who can provide "constructive conflict" and challenge you to change your mind (Heffernan, 2012). This can be built up through your cultural and management frameworks.

The power of no

Second thing you need to remember before you start your strategic planning is the power of the word 'no'. As a CEO, especially in a small organisation, you have to learn how to say no. Repeatedly. This can feel counterintuitive as you often feel the pressure to get as much business, as much attention, as much everything as you can get your hands on. You need the contacts. You need credibility. But saying yes to everything will not get you there. Saying yes to everything means you have more to do than a small organisation can cope with.

Which means everything will be done to a sub-par level, if it is done at all. And that is not how you build credibility. You focus on one to three things and you do them well. You do them better than any small organisation has a right to do them. Then people start paying attention and you can grow, and then start to take on more. Set yourself up for success by saying no.

As Steve Jobs said, "People think focus means saying yes to the thing you've got to focus on. But that's not what it means at all. It means saying no to the hundred other good ideas that there are. You have to pick carefully. I'm actually as proud of the things we haven't done as the things I have done. Innovation is saying no to 1,000 things." Or as Michael Porter, a leading academic in business strategy, put it more succinctly "The essence of strategy is choosing what not to do."

To identify what you need to say no to, consider the impact of saying yes on the three Ps: project, people, and patterns:
- What projects need to be put on hold if I say yes to this? Is this more important than those projects?
- Who will do the work if I say yes? Do they have enough capacity? Whose expectations will I need to manage?
- What behaviours and/or habits will need to change if I say yes? How long will new behaviours and/or habits take to form? (Bungay Stanier, 2016)

Recognise that everything you say yes to limits your ability to say yes to something else. Saying yes too much can lead to overload, burnout, and unkept promises. To ease the impact of the no, follow Bungay Stanier's (2016) advice: "say yes to the person, but say no to the task." Do not make the no personal, focus it on the task and detail the broad reasons behind the decision. A no does not have to be final, it can be a "no for now" which leaves the door open for a future yes when circumstances change.

Developing a strategy
The process of developing your strategy is highly valuable as it gives you time to pause and look up from your day-to-day toil. It allows you to see the wood for the trees. Even once you have developed your

strategy, you should regularly review it to give yourself the space to consider the context you are operating in and make sure your strategy continues to be relevant. All of this is expanded on below.

There is no defined amount of time that you need to spend developing your strategy. A strategy can be put together within a meeting, a month, or even a year, depending on how much effort is put into each step outlined below. The strategy will change and evolve as new information arises, so be open to feedback and do not be too precious about making changes. The process works best if one person takes the lead in developing the new strategy and is consistently involved in each step. Each step can be considered individually or as a group.

In a small organisation, it is recommended that you, as the CEO, collate the information on market analysis; community consultation; SWOT; vision, purpose, mission, aims, and values; and the moonshot target. Then arrange group meetings with your team and with your board to discuss the summaries of those steps, how they could be developed, and agree in principle; then break down the moonshot into overall objectives and targets for the coming strategic period. At this stage, you should individually draft the strategic plan and seek further feedback from the team and board to ensure you have accurately captured your discussions. After this stage, develop the operational plan and resources plan. Gather further feedback from the team and board on the feasibility of the strategic plan once the detail is understood. Finally, get it all signed off and start the easy part of enacting the plan and monitoring progress!

Market analysis
As a CEO, you should identify early on where you can find reliable, relevant, and useful information about the sector in which you are operating. Ask your team, your board, your communities, and your partners for recommendations. Sign up for all relevant newsletters, Google search updates, and read sector blogs at least on a weekly basis. Attend sector events, such as conferences. Create a research notes document and record any interesting and insightful information you come across, with reference and link to the source. Over a space of three months, this should give you a sufficiently detailed understanding of your sector to build out the market analysis for your

organisation. The research does not stop at the point of creating the analysis, you should continue to keep an eye on sector developments and update your analyses based on new information.

You must understand the external context in which you operate before you can evaluate your organisation and plan for the future. There are two main aspects to summarise the external context: a PESTLE analysis; and a five competitive forces analysis.

To structure a PESTLE (Political, Economic, Social, Technological, Legal, and Environmental) analysis: create a large table with the six categories and then break each category into what is relevant for (a) the work you do, (b) your organisation's operations, (c) the community you work with, and (d) the sector you work in. For example, under Legal, new HR requirements may not impact your services, the community you work with, or the sector you work in, but it will impact your operational arrangements internally. If there is a large environmental regulatory shift, your work and your organisation may already be compliant and thus unaffected but the community you work with may not be, which will have knock-on effects on the extent that they can engage with your work. When creating the table, focus solely on stating the facts and objective information as much as possible. Once all the information is sorted into the appropriate categories, review if any gaps indicate further research needs to be conducted.

Once you have a rounded list of information for each six categories, review them in turn, summarising the key facts with your opinion of why and how they will impact your organisation. Aim to keep the summary to one paragraph per sub-category so it is succinct and focused. This should then be presented back to your team and your board to check if they are aware of any information that is missing.

Another way to analyse your market is Porter's (2008) five competitive forces. This type of analysis helps define the barriers and/or competition your organisation may face in the external context. Consider the following forces:
1. Profit: how much profit/surplus are similar organisations making in your sector? How does your organisation

compare? If others are barely scraping by, what are the reasons behind that?

2. Customers: how large is your intended customer/client/service user market? How well served are they by competitors? Is there an unmet need? Is there a monopoly? Is the market saturated with choice? Do your customers have negotiating leverage over price?
3. Suppliers: are there suppliers that you will depend on? Are the suppliers powerful e.g. because there are few of them, they do not depend on your business, you face significant switching costs?
4. Potential entrants: Will profits draw others into the market? Is it easy to enter the market? Are there barriers to new entrants e.g. significant entry costs, economies of scale that favour incumbents, switching costs by customers, regulation?
5. Substitute products: are there substitutes to your service that fulfil the same need?

These will influence the competition your organisation will likely face in the market. As Porter (2008) outlines, competition will be intense if there are many competitors or all competitors are similar in size and power; growth is slow; exit barriers are high; competitors are motivated beyond economic performance; and there is a lack of transparency between competitors. Competition on price is likely to occur if the competitors' products/services are highly similar; costs of switching are low; fixed costs are high; organisational capacity can only grow in large increments; and the product is perishable. Through this analysis, you can identify whether there is space for your organisation within the market, where there is space, and how defendable that space is.

To work through this analysis, answer the questions above objectively based on your research. Summarise your findings with a paragraph on each competitive force and sense check it with your team and your board.

Community consultation
Alongside desk-based research, you should always connect with the community you seek to serve to understand their pains, gains, and desires from your organisation.

The different ways you could consult with your community:

- Meet and greets: attend existing events and service meetings attended by your community to engage in informal conversations and build trust.
  - Pros: people are relaxed and you can learn a lot through informal chat/building rapport and trust with your community / you can see the whole person and their whole experience rather than only focused on the questions you think are important
  - Cons: you have to limit your questions to avoid people feeling uncomfortable / conversations can veer off the relevant very easily / not very time efficient
- One-on-one interviews with representative members of your community: review the existing statistics about your community demographics to select people for the interview. Have a clear set of questions that you send them in advance so they feel comfortable and can prepare themselves for the experience.
  - Pros: you can get in-depth information
  - Cons: you make a lot of assumptions that they are representative and you only engage with known people who may already be engaged with your organisation
- Focus group: bring together a group of 6-8 people from your community, best engagement is when you add the focus group onto an existing event or service meeting.
  - Pros: less intimidating than an interview for the participants / unexpected but relevant tangents can emerge from discussion among participants
  - Cons: people can dominate the conversation/discussions take irrelevant turns
- 'Hackathon' style workshop: bring together a larger group of participants to identify solutions to a central question or problem (e.g. how your organisation should support the community). Structure the event around central questions, allowing participants to suggest discussion topics on Post-its and self-organise into groups to discuss the most interesting topics. Have them give feedback and then move on to the

next question. Encourage people to move between groups to where they feel they can add the most value.

- o Pros: Discussion is driven by the community around what they think is valuable / lots of ideas and suggestions can be generated in a short period of time
- o Cons: while the discussions are open, the event has to be very structured and it can be difficult to remain in control / Dominant personalities can take over discussions, just like in focus groups
- Survey your community: send out a virtual survey that should take no more than 5 to 10 minutes to complete.
  - o Pros: you will potentially receive a lot more responses than one-to-one interviews / people may be more honest if the survey is anonymised / it can be shared outside of your known community
  - o Cons: can be difficult to convince people to complete the survey, there is a general sense of survey fatigue

Ideally, your strategy will be informed by all of the above. Once you have collected feedback from your community, start identifying the central themes being repeated across responses. Be led by the data, rather than trying to find ways to fit the data with your preconceptions. Keep refining the categories down until they cannot be merged. This should inform the products/services your organisation looks to develop, as well as priorities based on community needs. It is likely that the community needs will focus on the following categories, as defined by Almquist and Bloch (2016) in their 'elements of value', based on Maslow's hierarchy of needs:

- Functional - value could be created by improving the tasks and activities that individuals need to fulfil in their day-to-day lives, such as a reduction in the required effort, time, cost; increased quality and/or variety; more information to make better decisions.
- Emotional - value can be created by eliciting positive emotional experiences such as joy, nostalgia, and wellness and/or reducing negative experiences such as anxiety, isolation, and anger.
- Life-changing - value could be created by enabling individuals to undergo positive transformation, such as providing hope

and motivation; a sense of belonging; and ability to pursue ambitions.
- Social impact - value could be created by connecting individuals with a sense of something greater than themselves.

Throughout all of your strategic thinking and planning, you should sense check your objectives and targets against your community consultation. Ask yourself:
- Do your plans align with the needs of your community?
- Are you alleviating their pains?
- Are you achieving their gains?
- Is your planned delivery accessible to members of your community?

Where your plans do not align with the community's needs, explore whether those objectives and targets are necessary. Always consider what value will be generated. If you cannot identify the value, then you need to rework the plan or scrap it entirely. These questions, along with your plan, will form the basis of your organisational value proposition.

SWOT analysis

Based on your market analysis and community consultation, you can start to complete your SWOT (Strengths, Weaknesses, Opportunities, and Threats) analysis. This allows you to review a snapshot of your organisation against the external context.

Start by completing the Opportunities and Threats columns, based on your market analysis and community consultation. Opportunities arise in the external context that may benefit your organisation and your ability to implement your plans. Threats (as the name implies) threaten your organisation and your plans.

Then review what strengths you have in the organisation to take advantage of the opportunities and mitigate the threats. Likewise, what weaknesses exist in the organisation that create barriers to accessing the opportunities and increase the risks of the threats.

Vision, mission, aims, and values

Regardless of where you are in your organisational development, setting your vision, mission, and aims should come after your market and SWOT analyses. If you are starting completely from scratch, you will have a dream or a general sense of your vision and aims to direct your analysis. Especially in that early stage, that vision will grow, evolve, and pivot as you learn more about the context in which you operate. You will understand more about where your strengths and weaknesses lie relative to the external environment, which will help you zero in on the value you could create through your organisation. The earlier you are in your organisational development, the more likely it will be that you will need to cycle through market analysis, SWOT, and vision setting as you refine your idea. If your organisation is fairly well developed, you'll maybe only go through one or two cycles.

The vision is the central cause of why you are doing what you are doing. As Simon Sinek (2011) has argued, the vision is the north star for the organisation. Without it, it is very easy for everyone (including you as a leader) to disassociate, drift from focus, put in the minimum effort required to get through each day, and cruise along collecting payslips. A good way to set your vision is to imagine what the world would look like to put you out of business. This will help focus your vision on creating value for the benefit of society. Remember, if you do achieve your vision, it does not mean that you have to go out of business. It'll be a sign that you need a new vision. Summarise that vision in a sentence, using vocabulary that will allow others to understand the 'why' behind your organisation. For example, your vision may be "a world without hunger".

Your organisation is unlikely to achieve this vision by itself. There will be a host of other organisations, government bodies, private individuals, etc that will have their roles to play in achieving the overall vision. Therefore, you need to identify your 'mission statement'. While your vision is your 'why', your mission statement is your 'how'; how your organisation will contribute to achieving the vision. Following on from the above example, your mission statement may be "We create healthy, affordable meals for families and carers".

Next, you break that mission statement down into the 2 to 4 main areas in which you work to form your 'aims'. These describe what you do day-to-day. Continuing the above example, your aims may be "(1) Work with nutritionists, chefs, medical professionals, and child development experts to create healthy and varied meal plans. (2) Partner with supermarkets to offer nutritious meal deals. (3) Run training sessions in schools and community groups to raise awareness of healthy eating." Through this process, you funnel your vision down into actionable objectives which can be easily understood by internal and external stakeholders. All of your messaging and communications can then be crafted around these central statements (see part 3 in 'Communications').

Finally, you need to identify the values with which you will carry out your aims. This will later influence your work on developing the organisational culture in a way that aligns with your organisational strategy. Think of your values as the attributes you would like your partners to list when someone asks them to describe your organisation. This is not a lofty set of ideals, your values will be integrated into all work that you do and will help define what 'good' looks like for your strategy, your work, and your team. They can and should be integrated into everything you do.

Some useful exercises to define your values:
1. Do an online search for a list of organisational values - there are many pages with hundreds of adjectives. Read through the list to identify the top 20 you identify with. Then review those 20 to see if any themes or clusters emerge. Keep categorising until you end up with the 3 to 5 most important that capture the essence of your top 20.
2. If you are starting a new organisation: brainstorm the adjectives you would like future partners to use when giving you feedback about your work. Compare this list against the list generated in exercise 1 - if they are different, refine your list of 3-5 values further.
3. If you are in an established organisation: review the feedback you receive from your partners and your community. Identify key themes that emerge in how they describe your organisation. Compare this list against the list generated in exercise 1 - if they are different, reflect on why there is a

difference. Are you falling short of your ideals? Does the feedback reflect values you had not considered? Refine your list of 3 to 5 values further.

Moonshot target

Once you have a clear understanding of why your organisation exists, what it intends to focus on, and how it intends to behave, you can start to distil your strategy for the next few years. Start by defining a moonshot target. The importance of translating your vision into a moonshot target is best summed up by this quote from Kets de Vries (1994): "One should never forget that a vision without action is a form of hallucination."

The moonshot should be achievable and serve to rally your team around a central target. Further to the previous example, your moonshot target may be "By 2030, we will have supported 1 million families". The timeline for the target should be approximately three strategic cycles in the future. For example, if you are brand new and you can barely see one year into the future, then put your moonshot three years into the future. If you are well-established and operate on a three-year cycle, put your moonshot ten years into the future. Scale as appropriate for you. Once you have that central target, add in some detail about what success looks like. This three-cycle moonshot lets you dream big, while still maintaining a sense of what is practically achievable.

Strategic plan

Next, break your moonshot down into the key areas you need to focus on in each of your three strategic cycles. While quite broad, it should still give you a sense of how each cycle will build on the preceding one, leading towards your moonshot.

Finally, consider your first strategic cycle to identify the key targets and key actions that you will need to take across this defined time period. There are multiple ways to approach thinking this through:

- Break each of your organisational aims into the projects and work streams that lie behind it. Consider how these will need to be developed to contribute to your moonshot target.

- Consider each stakeholder that you need to work with and how you will work with them over the strategic cycle.

Beyond referring back to your vision, purpose, mission, aims, values, and moonshot, avoid limiting the brainstorming around strategic targets. Keep checking with your group if there are any gaps missing in relation to the above categories. You will likely end up with an impossibly long list of targets and actions that need to be taken. That's good.

The next step is to filter and focus. Start by grouping the ideas around their commonalities and themes, as you did with your organisational values. Keep filtering and focusing until you have around 3-5 themes of key targets. Order the actions under these targets according to priority and closest fit with your organisational aims. Building on this, think about the timings of each action - is there a chronological sequence for certain actions? What needs to be done first? Approximately how long will the actions take?

Finally, consider what your measures of success will be for each key target and key actions. You must have a clear sense of what 'good' looks like and how you will measure whether the target has been achieved.

It is a good idea to build this initial strategic plan in a spreadsheet, with columns for your key targets, key actions, year (or another strategic time period) to be achieved, review point, and measure of success. Keep track of your targets by assigning them numerical values that can then be broken into sub-points so you can see how each action links back up to the target.

Coming back to the example, the moonshot target of "By 2030, we will have supported 1 million families" could have Aim 1: Cookbook with weekly meal plans and recipes / Target 1.1: Create 52 weekly meal plans / Action 1.1.1 Build relationships with child nutritionists. This will make it much easier to expand on each aim, target, and action as you develop your operational plan.

Operational plan

The operational plan breaks the strategic plan down into smaller and smaller chunks to identify the sub-actions that will need to be achieved, who will be responsible for each sub-action, and their timescales for achievement. At this point, it is a good idea to create a separate tab in your spreadsheet, copying over your strategic plan and adding columns for sub-actions; responsible team member(s); year (refined to each sub-action); deadline/review point (refined to each sub-action); and a colour coding with which you will be able to monitor progress.

By doing this in a spreadsheet, you can then add filters to your column to review the plan for each year and/or each team member. This will help you better visualise the strategy to understand its feasibility. It is common to bunch all of the targets into the first strategic sub-period (e.g. quarter, year) as we get excited and want to achieve quick wins. However, that tends to overload the team and leave little room for flexibility or the ability to react to contextual changes. Unless your strategy calls for significant growth, it is best to split the strategy into equal parts and look to deliver a consistent amount each year.

In putting together the operational plan, consider the interdependencies between your strategic targets. It is likely there will be a chronological order to the targets - some may need to be completed before other targets can be started. Others may be most efficient to complete concurrently where they make use of the same resources and knowledge gained from each target can enhance the other. You also need to consider external factors in your operational plan, for example, funders may demand work be completed within a set timescale and thus need to be prioritised over internal projects.

Once you have your operational plan drafted, you can move on to build your resources plan and truly understand how realistic your strategic plan is.

Resources plan
Each strategic plan should be reviewed against the following resources:
- Human - do you have enough team members to deliver the plan? Do you have the right skills in your team to deliver the plan? Do you have an appropriate management structure to support the plan? If not, you will need to add to your

operational plan details of how you will upskill your existing team; recruit additional team members; help existing team members move on; restructure.

- Cultural - does your organisational culture fit with your plan? How will you motivate and support your team to integrate the new vision and moonshot target? More on culture in the next section.
- Financial - do you have sufficient income sources to fund the plan? How will you fundraise; build your sales pipeline; grow your existing income sources to enable your plan?
- Physical - do you have the workspace, infrastructure, machinery, etc to achieve your plan? What do you need to acquire? What are the timescales associated with that acquisition and how will that impact your plan's timescales?
- Social - do you need external partnerships; brand recognition; community engagement, etc to achieve your plan? How will you go about building these connections? How long will that take? How will that impact your plan?
- Technological - do you have access to the technology you need to achieve the plan? If not, how will you create/licence the necessary technology?

As you explore these categories, you will need to further refine your strategic and operational plan. You will likely cycle through the strategic, operational, and resource planning stages a few times as you solidify your realistic plan. There is no point in setting an unachievable strategic plan. Include stretch goals by all means to motivate people. But setting people up to fail is unacceptable. Setting unachievable goals will not motivate, it will alienate and discourage.

Having a clear sense of how the strategic, operational, and resource plans support each other will help your team understand how they personally contribute to organisational success. It will also help you where an unexpected external influence derails your strategy, such as a global pandemic, or an unexpected opportunity arises that you feel compelled to pursue. If it knocks out a target, you will see how that ultimately impacts your team's workload, your revenue requirements, and even your training priorities. You can make informed choices on how to react.

Presenting strategy

You will likely need to present your strategy within a broader business plan document. The foundations of this should start with a business model canvas, as designed by Osterwalder. Complete the canvas in the following order:

- Value proposition and customer segments: what value are you intending to deliver to who?
- Customer relationships and channels: what type of relationships are you intending to build with your customers/clients/service users and how are you going to reach them?
- Key activities and key resources: what will you need to do to deliver your value proposition and what resources do you need to be able to deliver it?
- Key partners: who (external to your organisation) needs to be involved to enable you to deliver your value proposition?
- Revenue streams and cost structure: how will you generate the income to deliver your value proposition?

Once visualised, you will need to fill out each section to form your business plan. You will need to cover the following headings within your business plan:

- Executive summary: write at the end to summarise everything else
- Organisation summary: vision, mission, aims, values, legal entity
- Market need: customer segments and their jobs, pains, and gains
- Value proposition: the services/products you intend to supply to alleviate your customer pains and achieve your customer gains
- Market analysis: PESTLE, SWOT, community consultation, five competitive forces analysis demonstrating how you are best placed to deliver the value proposition
- Strategic plan: summary of your key activities for the strategic period
- Resources plan: outline the resources you have to achieve the strategic plan, what you need to develop, and how you will develop additional resources

- Financial plan: separate out how you will generate the revenue to deliver your value proposition. This will link to a hefty financial projections spreadsheet where you will need to calculate and project ahead each time on your balance sheet. Note each assumption you make through the calculation for future reference.

Think of this document as a contingency in case you become incapacitated. In summarising all of the above, it should contain the key reasons behind the decisions that you make. Your successor should be able to read it, understand your logic, and continue your plan without any hesitation. Or rip it up and write a completely new plan, as successors are oft to do.

Monitoring strategy

Once you have your strategy, you need to build in regular review points with the team to agree on objectives, check in, and measure progress. Without objectives and check-ins, the strategy will slide into obscurity. Without clear deadlines and progress markers, work will expand to fill all the available time, in line with Parkinson's law. As an aside, you will also need to integrate your strategy into all policies and processes outlined in Part 3: Operations.

The very practical approach to integrating this monitoring into an organisation and into a team is the OKR approach. OKR stands for Objectives and Key Results. Objectives are "WHAT is to be achieved", while Key Results are "HOW we get to the objective" (Doerr, 2018). By definition when the key results are achieved, the objective is achieved. The strategic and operational plan should be translated into quarterly discussions within the team to identify the objectives and key results for that period. As part of this planning session, run "pre-mortems" to identify ways the team could go wrong to implement mitigating actions at the start (Pink, 2019). The central team OKRs can then be cascaded down to each team member's own list of OKRs. At the end of each quarter, the team should collectively review progress, grade their achievements, identify key learnings and improvements, and then set their OKRs for the next quarter.

OKRs are useful as they clearly define what is expected of each person; everyone has a sense of how they contribute to the bigger picture; and it allows each person to prioritise and effectively manage their time. Everyone has ownership. Everyone understands the WHY. Everyone is involved and so they feel motivated to see it through. The regular review points also allow for continuous improvement and learning to be built into the team. The team should review the reasons behind objectives' achievement and non-achievement, to identify improvements that can be made for the future, additional training and/or support that is required, and additional resources that need to be put in place.

As John Doerr warns, OKRs should not be used as a weapon against team members, they should be used as a yardstick against which the team can measure their performance and track progress. Where OKRs are aspirational, make that clear so the team knows to strive but do not see themselves as failures if they do not accomplish the stretch goals. OKRs are only useful as long as they are relevant to the strategy and measure appropriate outcomes. They should be treated flexibly and you should be ready and able to pivot if their relevance ceases.

At the end of each year, the team should review the year as a whole. It can be useful to structure the review around the following questions:
- What was our goal/intention with [project]?
- What went well? What was good practice?
- With hindsight, what could have gone better? How could we be better? What are the areas for improvement?
- What are the key learnings?
- What will be carried forward?

As CEO, reflect on these questions ahead of the meeting and capture your thoughts. Then facilitate the team in reflecting on the above questions. Allow the team to speak first before you add your thoughts to avoid creating an echo chamber and stifling divergent comments. This will also build your team's reflective skills, which will enable them to learn and grow in their individual activities as well.

As part of the review, make note of the OKRs achieved, and the impact on the subsequent year's strategic and operational plans. The strategic and operational plans should be updated to reflect progress and then broken down into OKRs once again every quarter. This monitoring process enables the strategic and operational plans to evolve and grow with the organisation, rather than remaining static.

Culture

Whenever people come together in a group, a culture will organically emerge. There will be ways things are done. There will be ways people think. Boundaries will emerge on what is acceptable and what is unacceptable. Reinforcement and punishment behaviours will evolve, traditions and rituals will become ingrained, and people will be conditioned to abide by the culture's expectations or be forced out.

Every individual has influence over the culture; it is in constant flux and can grow with its members. The extent to which someone can influence the culture depends on the level of power ascribed to them by the culture. In a workplace, cultural power does not necessarily align with a person's role and responsibilities. The CEO may be seen as a figurehead, while the Deputy is the real influencer. The longest-serving staff member may be looked to for approval on proposed changes, or they may be viewed as a deadweight that keeps the organisation back from its potential.

As CEO, it is your role to ensure that the organisational culture serves the vision and strategy of the organisation. In a brand new organisation, it is your role to set the foundation to encourage the emergence of the right culture for the organisation's goals. As a CEO of an established organisation, it is your role to influence cultural change towards what is required.

Defining culture

According to the cultural dynamics model (Hatch, 1993) in the academic literature, culture is made up of four facets:
- Assumptions: the baseline "correct" way of doing things e.g. "we don't do it like that here"
- Values: how things "ought to be" e.g. "we do this because we think it is friendly and this organisation is friendly"
- Artefacts: how the culture is enacted e.g. people's behaviours, organisational policies and procedures, communication methods
- Symbols: how the culture is represented e.g. branding, office decor, case studies

These four facets influence each other in an endless cycle - assumptions define values, which directs behaviours, which shapes symbols, which can be interpreted to build assumptions. The same is true in reverse - symbols influence behaviours, which lead to the interpretation of underlying values, which shapes assumptions, which creates symbols. As Hatch (1993) explained, culture undergoes "successive revisions of interpretations of social phenomena as each new level of understanding calls for revision of the basis on which that understanding is grounded".

As a CEO, you need to be aware of these four facets and their interactions if you wish to understand the organisation's culture and influence a change.

Guiding cultural change

Start first with an honest analysis of the cultural facets of the organisation. There is often misalignment between the organisational symbols and artefacts, and the underlying values and assumptions. For example, an office can be decorated with photos of smiling beneficiaries, a website full of heart-warming case studies, and policies filled with statements about putting the beneficiary at the heart of the organisation, but the underlying assumptions and values are that financial growth is supreme and all actual organisational activity is the cold-hearted pursuit of income. Cultural webs and audits can be useful to map the different facets of the organisation. You need to be aware of what exists before you start to map how to achieve your new cultural goals.

Cultural change is not easy and it is not quick. Both the organisation and the people within it will demonstrate homeostatic resistance (O'Neill, 2007) to change; they will want to preserve the existing internal environment from a force of habit, regardless of how dysfunctional it might be. There are set circumstances that are more receptive to leaders' actions on cultural change. Borrowing from the terminology of contingency theorists, leadership change activities take more hold in 'weak' circumstances, as opposed to 'strong'. In strong circumstances, there is uniformity in the interpretation of concepts and clarity in how to respond to certain situations. In contrast, in weak circumstances, there is confusion and a lack of interpretation about a situation and its implications (Tsui et al., 2006). In such circumstances, CEOs are more able to impose their own interpretations, values, and garner support around a well-articulated vision. In strong situations, it is likely the CEO's efforts will be overlooked or even actively resisted.

Attempting to enforce a completely new culture will be rejected immediately by the organisation and the team. The cultural audit will reveal the current cultural facets and how they are integrated with the power structures, organisational structures, and control systems. It is likely that certain assumptions and values can be repurposed for the new culture.

If you feel cultural change is required, it is good to start embedding it around a time of strategic change. As described in the Strategy section, a key part of strategic planning is defining the organisational values for the upcoming strategic period. Involving the team in this stage will let them feel more ownership of the new culture and increase their openness to the change. Depending on the size of your team, those involved with defining the new culture may need to be supported to become role models of the new culture within the wider organisation. You will need to collectively agree on the behaviours they will demonstrate and encourage among colleagues. Consistency is crucial.

You will then need to systematically review the artefacts and symbols in the organisation to align them with the newly defined values. This will subliminally prompt employees to evolve their cultural assumptions and values. This will likely involve reviewing and amending the following:
- All written policies and procedures
- Appraisal, reward, team building, and management systems
- Physical spaces, such as the office layout, decoration, furniture
- Communication materials such as logos, annual reports, and websites

Depending on the level of deviation from the previous culture, you may wish to consider some way to symbolise the cultural change within the wider organisation. Howard-Grenville et al (2011) discovered from their empirical research that leaders can use 'liminal' moments to bracket the everyday and work with employees to embrace alternative approaches and interpretations of artefacts. These liminal moments could take the form of team building sessions that are focused on the new values of the culture. For example, if one of your values is fearlessness, you could organise a team hot coals walking experience. Supportiveness could involve trust exercises. Collaboration could be an escape room. Give your team the space to experience and model the new behaviours outside of their day-to-day work environment. It will feel more familiar and safe back in the office, and the new team dynamics will have started to form.

Facets of positive working culture

As previously stated, the definition of a good working culture is set by the organisation's strategy. However, there are elements of a positive working culture that will be applicable to all organisations as it is linked to factors that help people thrive. The central tenet is that everyone is treated with respect. Do not compromise on this.

You should ensure that the following exist as a baseline, around which the rest of your culture can be built:

- Bullying and harassment are not tolerated and are immediately addressed through management systems. This applies to employees, partners, beneficiaries, everyone.
- People are allowed to maintain their dignity wherever possible. If something embarrassing happens, you do not mock. If they are fired, you discuss how it will be communicated with the wider team and public (if applicable).
- People are listened to and their thoughts are considered. You do not need to act on everything, but you do not dismiss without hearing a word.
- People are supported to achieve their full potential at work. You invest in training and learning.

Facets of negative working culture

Following on from the above, you can spot a negative working culture the moment that people are not shown respect. It does not matter how successful the organisation appears, if people are not treated with respect it is a sign of a dysfunctional culture. Imagine how much more successful the organisation would be if it had a healthy culture.

Dysfunctional cultures can evolve out of behaviours that go unchecked. Michael Bungay Stanier outlined the "seven dysfunctional dwarves" that can emerge within teams: Sulky, Moany, Shouty, Crabby, Martyr-r, Touchy, and Petulant (Bungay Stanier, 2016). If team members see others portraying these behaviours and not being reprimanded (or worse, the dysfunctional team member is seen to be rewarded), then it builds the assumption that such behaviour is acceptable and the value that this is how they ought to behave as well. As CEO, you should actively avoid displaying any of the above behaviour.

Dysfunctional cultures can also evolve out of team members adopting one of the following three archetypal roles: Victim, Persecutor, and Rescuer (Bungay Stanier, 2016). Each is just as unhelpful and dysfunctional as the other. The Victim forgoes all sense of personal responsibility and sees everything as being "done to them". The Persecutor similarly forgoes all sense of personal responsibility and attacks those around them for any and all issues, pressuring them to take on personal responsibility. And the Rescuer takes on the personal responsibility of all those around them, trying to fix everything and depriving others of having personal responsibility. Those portraying these roles will need to be coached to understand the underlying assumptions and habits that trigger the person to slide into these unhelpful roles and to find ways of reclaiming their personal responsibility.

CEOs often take on the role of the Rescuer, which results in a codependent team and an overwhelmed CEO. It can be easy to fall into the trap of thinking it is just quicker and better to solve team members' issues. But that is actually a form of disrespect towards your team, as you both assume they cannot deal with their own problems and you remove an opportunity for them to learn. And a lack of respect is a clear sign of a dysfunctional culture.

Your management structures will play a key role in identifying, addressing, and ultimately stamping out dysfunctional behaviours.

This will serve to improve the working culture and guide the embedding of your cultural change.

Management

Management structures, approaches, policies, and procedures should be built around the organisational strategy and intended culture. As a CEO, management will be a key part of your role. It may be the most impactful part of your role on a day-to-day basis. You are likely going to be a few tiers removed from the actual work of the organisation, and therefore your value can be found in being a multiplier for your team: enabling them to fulfil their potential and deliver. Management should be viewed as a vital and central part of your role. It is not an afterthought, a nice-to-have if there is time available, or a drain on your time. If you have spent your day in meetings with your team members, removing obstacles and supporting them with their work, then that is a successful day. Give management the respect it deserves. Your team will thank you for it and the organisation will thank you for it.

When you consider managing people, remember that jobs are not eternal. People will leave their jobs and that is a good thing, both for the person and the organisation. People should only stay in a job as long as they are the best person for the job AND that job is the best job for that person. A person is not entitled to their job and you as CEO are not entitled to that person. You both have to be right for the other. You are a team, not a family.

When you accept that people can and will move on (be it to a different job, to education, to their family, to retire, etc), you will allow yourself to be more objective in evaluating their suitability; making tough decisions; and reacting to them leaving.

Managing an effective team
Intentions and expectations
Make your intentions and expectations clear: for the organisation, for the team, for each team member. There is a highly useful term all CEOs need to be familiar with: confabulation. This is where people "replace missing information with something false [they] believe to be true" (Brown, 2018). When people do not know what was intended or what is expected, they fill in the gaps for themselves. Each person

will fill the gap in a slightly different way, leading to confusion, disagreements, and disorder.

You will need to set your intentions and expectations in the following ways:

- Acceptable behaviours: you will need a staff handbook that outlines what acceptable behaviours look like within the organisation. Where there are tasks and procedures that are regularly repeated, you may want to create a handbook to standardise performance.
- Roles and responsibilities: job descriptions, organisational charts, work splits, and annual targets should be regularly reviewed to keep them relevant. People need to know the structures within which they are operating. This does not inherently stifle innovation and creativity. Where limits are not defined, people can get lost in opportunities and can struggle to focus.
- Project briefs: clarify the aims of each new project, how it fits with the broader strategic plan, set the responsibilities of each team member in accordance with RACI (Responsible, Accountable, Consulted, and Informed), and agree on the intended outcomes.
- Meeting structures: you do not necessarily need a formal agenda for each meeting. But the aims of the meeting and the intended outcomes should be communicated prior to the meeting and at the start so everyone involved can understand what is expected of them.
- Team building and socialising: it is important for high functioning professional relationships that team members relate to each other as individuals. You can define clear socialising time with collective lunches, team building activities, and drinks after work. These need to be defined as work-based socialising so that people remember that they need to maintain a certain level of professionalism. This is not the time to get drunk and hit on colleagues. The HR policies and procedures that govern behaviour during work hours still apply - it is just an opportunity to talk about and do something other than work tasks together.

Having clear intentions and expectations is especially important if staff are working remotely. Spontaneous conversations and discussions are less likely to take place when people are not in a room together. You need to be intentional with your communications, making it clear when different discussions will take place, and capturing the outcomes of discussions afterwards. You cannot rely on the word getting around, so you need to intentionally message or virtually meet with each member of the team so they all receive the same information at the same time.

You also need to be intentional with your team socialisation. People do not socialise in the same way when working remotely. You rarely call up a colleague to ask how their weekend was or how they are settling in with their new pet. Therefore, you need to intentionally build in social time and set out clear expectations of behaviour during social time. It can be valuable to schedule a weekly half an hour where no one is allowed to talk about work. There can be a general chat or structured fun (e.g. games that work well virtually like Pictionary, online board games, quizzes) that allow team members to unwind and connect with one another. Team meetings can start with 5 to 10 minutes of open conversation before you start on the agenda items.

Create a positive working environment

It is important to make the work environment one that you enjoy. You are spending around half of your waking hours during the week at work so you should make it an environment that is pleasant to be in. Paint the walls. Put up pictures. Build in joyful moments that unite your team. Make it fun. Ignore for a second all the benefits that it brings to the team, their motivation, and their improved productivity. Do it for you. Do it because you only live your life once. Do it because you deserve to have a happy environment during those 40 hours per week. (If you are spending significantly more time at work than 40 hours, refer back to the Boundaries section in Part 1.)

The mental health statistics back this up. Research has shown that mental health problems affect one in six British workers each year and mental health is now the leading cause of sickness absence. The annual cost of poor mental health to employers is between £33 billion and £44 billion. This cost arises from presenteeism where individuals are at work but significantly less productive due to poor mental health, as well as from sickness absence and staff turnover (Farmer, 2017).

As part of creating a positive work environment, you will need to protect the health, safety, and wellbeing of your team. It's worth creating a staff wellbeing policy that incorporates the six core standards of the Thriving at Work guidance (which sets out best practice for supporting staff wellbeing) and the six principles of the HSE's Management Standards (which outlines the six main areas of work design that can alleviate work-related stress). More on this in Part 3.

Recruitment

When you realise there is a gap in your team, take the time to reflect on:

- The ideal split of tasks within your existing team: it is possible (extremely likely in a small organisation) that existing team members are weighed down by tasks that are unrelated to their main role but they have taken on because the work needs to get done by someone. When you sort the irrelevant tasks, you will likely end up with a whole new role (or more) that you ideally might want to recruit. A word of warning - do not just assume people will want to give up work, it may be that they really enjoy their irrelevant tasks. Work with them to support them in giving up the work or even encourage them to apply to the new position if it turns out all of their enjoyable tasks should be taken away.
- The ideal skills and behaviours the ideal employee would have to flourish in the new role. If you have high performing employees in similar roles, reflect on what skills and behaviours they demonstrate you would like more of. Conversely, if you have low performers, reflect on the areas of improvement you are working with them on and look to hire someone with those skills.
- The ideal skill and knowledge mix you would want within your organisation. Especially within a small organisation, each new hire can bring new skills beyond what is required for their role that can fill a gap. Reflect on the existing skills and knowledge to identify that gap.

Based on these reflections, put together a job description and person specification. As previously mentioned, the job description makes your intention clear and should help keep applicants focused. The person specification communicates your expectations. Your person specification will form the foundation of your scorecard for each stage of interviewing, so make sure it is highly relevant and targeted. Remove anything superfluous like the standard 'educated to a degree level'. Why do they need to be educated to a degree level? Are you in fact wanting someone who can demonstrate analytical thinking, problem-solving skills, and an ability to process high levels of information? Reflect on the language used to keep it inclusive.

Unconscious bias is real and can emerge in unexpected ways. Do not underestimate it. Build in structures at the start of the application process to try to remove as much bias as possible. Consider the appropriateness of the following:

- Anonymised applications - have a standard application form that has been designed in an accessible format that has sections for all relevant information. Why ask for a cover letter that can be interpreted (or misinterpreted) by different cultural experiences? If you have initial questions the cover letter should cover, just ask the questions in the application form. Do away with CVs: they are just marketing materials. The first section of the application form should ask for identifiable information so you can contact applications about the outcome of their applications. Ask an employee not involved in the application process to remove this page and assign an anonymised marker to the application before forwarding it to the recruiting team.
- Have a shortlisting scoring system - assign each applicant a score against each item on the person specification. Depending on the importance of each item, you may wish to assign weightings to better reflect your needs. Set a minimum score required for interviewing before you look at any candidates. Ideally, have more than one person complete the scoring to reduce the impact of individual biases. Jointly review those candidates who have scored enough to be invited to interview. If you have too many eligible candidates, consider whether you can put on additional interview days. If

you cannot, then set a higher score threshold and filter until you are left with only the best ones you can interview. If you do not have any above your interview threshold, do not settle. Review your person specification, the job description, and the places you advertised, and refine the process. Open applications again - do not settle. A mediocre performer will harm your existing team as they will pull down standards, make the rest frustrated or complacent, and they will eventually leave anyway as the role was not right for them. Better to spend a longer time recruiting, than years cursing your recruitment choices.

- Have multiple interviewers on the interview panel - try to select a diverse group, both in terms of the protected characteristics and also in life experiences. This should balance out unconscious biases across the group and minimise groupthink.
- As with the applications, have a scoring system against each interview question and have standardised questions. You can add clarifying questions based on the applications, but these should not receive scores. Consider sharing the interview questions with candidates ahead of time, to support those who have anxiety, accessibility needs, and/or neurodiversity.
- Build in an exercise in which the candidate can demonstrate key skills and/or behaviours required for the role. For example, an improvised client call; a written exercise; a presentation. Again, these should have a scoring system and each member of the interview panel should score the outcome.
- Finally, where possible, allow the candidates to spend time with members of their team. This benefits both sides. The team can be given an opportunity to ask their specific questions (again - ask them to score independently) and it allows the candidate to see if there is a cultural fit with their potential colleagues.

Once all the scoring has been completed, gather all those involved in the interviewing process and identify the candidates with the highest scores. Then go around one by one to ask each interviewer 'yes' or 'no' to the final candidate. Unanimous decisions are preferable - prioritising the views of those who will have to work with the person (if your organisation is big enough that everyone does not work with everyone). Hesitancy or undecidedness cannot be allowed. Each new team member can have a potentially enormous impact on the organisation, regardless of its size. Make a decision and commit to it.

Once a decision is made, tell the candidate as soon as possible. Communicate your enthusiasm for them, equal to the enthusiasm you expect from them. Always make the offer subject to references. While past performance is not predictive of future performance, red flags should always be considered. As you collect references of the candidate, consider how you can provide references to the candidate of your organisation. A good idea can be an informal meeting with their new team, again to review the cultural fit and make sure everyone feels like they will be able to work with each other. This can also serve as one of your first steps towards that individual's induction as their first day will not involve walking into a room of unfamiliar faces.

All of this is time intensive, but worth it if you can hire the best person for your job. A high performer will more than pay back the investment within their first year.

Induction and integration

As repeatedly said throughout, if you invest adequate time and energy to get things right at the start, it will pay dividends in the long term. That is especially true when inducting someone into your organisation. A person's induction should include the following:

- Legal requirements - terms of their contract, health and safety around the workplace, HR policies and procedures, line management arrangements, and the expectations of them as an employee of the organisation.
- Vision, strategy, and how it relates to them - inspire them with the organisation's vision, the journey the organisation is on, and how they will personally contribute to the achievement of that vision and journey.
- Organisational culture - outline to them the facets of the organisation's culture: the assumptions, values, behaviours, artefacts, symbols, and traditions of the place. Give them the

knowledge and tools to be able to adapt and fit into this new environment.

- Team building - give them time with each member of their new team to understand how their roles fit together and also to understand them as a fellow person. Building familiarity and trust with colleagues early on will encourage the new person to ask questions rather than sitting scared at their desk unsure of what to do.
- Context setting - outline to them the different streams of work that exist in the team / department / organisation so they can understand the context in which they will be working. If they understand why they do what they do in their role, they will learn much faster and can start to make suggestions on improvements early on.
- Task teaching - the final thing an induction should focus on is the actual day-to-day tasks the person will be required to fulfil. Shadowing colleagues, demonstrations, discrete pieces of work can build this knowledge and the person's confidence to be allowed to take on work independently.

A comprehensive induction tends to last around four weeks (for full-time staff). The first week should begin with a mix of top-level descriptions mixed with team building and small tasks to allow for mental breaks, e.g. setting up their workstation, reading key policies, exploring the intranet / file systems. The second week should start to bring in context setting, further team building, and some initial task teaching, again recognising the fatigue that can come from learning lots of new information. Small discrete tasks should be given so the person can learn a bit by doing. Finally, the third week should lead to the introduction of actual work and responsibilities, and the easing of the intensity of the induction. Their fourth week should be close to a normal week, allowing them to put in place their learning and take their first tentative steps as a new, productive employee.

As a line manager, you should ease back on the intensity of your line management with each passing week. In the first week, you should meet with the new employee at the start and end of each day to give them time to reflect and ask questions. In the second week, it will likely be sufficient to only meet at the start of each day. Be led by the employee's needs. In the third week, every other day will seem sufficient, especially as they will be receiving direct support from other colleagues throughout each day as part of their task teaching sessions. In the fourth week, transition to a more usual weekly one-to-one meeting, with ad hoc support given as requested. Consider the process like teaching them to ride a bike. In the first week, you are just showing them the bike, getting them comfortable with the idea of riding a bike. In the second week, they have taken a seat and you are firmly holding the bike to get them used to balancing. In the third week, they have started to pedal and you are holding the seat to steady them. In the fourth week, you release the seat gently and jog along as they pedal away, a bit unsteady. From then on, you watch as they pedal away and stay within shouting range in case they run into trouble.

At the end of the four weeks, it is good to schedule a team celebration/team building session. This builds on the idea of liminality, mentioned within the culture section. The end of the formal induction can be seen as the traditional ritual of transition from adolescence into adulthood. A team social acts as the ritual to welcome the new employee as a full member of the team. A structured activity with a sense of achievement is best, as opposed to a solely social activity like going for dinner, as it will unite the team around the goal and give them a common experience around which to build in-jokes. Some examples are quizzes, escape rooms, and cocktail making. Going for a meal afterwards helps build in more informal social time, where the new bonds can be deepened. This mirrors traditional rituals, which are usually followed by a feast of some kind. It's worked for thousands of years and will work to fully induct and integrate your new employee.

Team dynamics

A team is not a family. A team comes together around a common purpose, to achieve a common goal. Team members want to be together, they are together based on choice. Team members are selected based on their ability to contribute; if they do not live up to their role, they are removed from the team. There can be a deep connection and sense of caring between team members, but the common purpose and goal supersede all else. Individual differences are put aside in pursuit of the common interest. Cultivate a team, not a family, for your organisation.

Building on all of the other aforementioned elements in building an effective team, the following five factors need to be in place (Schmidt et al., 2020):

- **Safety** - psychological safety is required for team members to explore their thoughts, implement their ideas, and take appropriate risks. This is based on trust and mutual respect between team members. Michael Bungay Stanier outlines four primary drivers for a situation to feel safe or dangerous (1) Tribe - "are you with me or against me?" If someone feels they are part of a team and have the support of those around them, they will feel safe; (2) Expectation - "do I know the future or don't I?" Where people know what is expected and can anticipate outcomes of actions, they will feel safe; (3) Rank - "what is my role in relation to others?" When people know where they stand, they will feel comfortable and behave in accordance with the power dynamics; and (4) Autonomy - "do I get a say or don't I?" Autonomy will build a sense of safety in that people feel their needs can be communicated, heard, and acted upon. If they do not get a say, they will feel overlooked and undervalued, and they will disengage.
- **Clarity** - this has already been covered under 'intentions and expectations'. When requirements are clearly communicated, teams will be more effective in delivering outcomes.
- **Meaning** - each team member should believe that they make a meaningful contribution to the overall team and they should know how their actions contribute. This can be achieved through the organisational strategic and operational plan, which funnels the overall organisation vision down to the individual level. That way, each individual knows how they fit with the whole and how their actions influence the outcomes of those around them.
- **Dependability** - Team members need to be able to rely on each other to do what they say they will do. Team members need to be transparent with their actions, keep colleagues up-to-date with developments, and be responsive to each other. This applies to the CEO as well. According to Daniel Pink (2019), email response time is the single best predictor of whether employees are satisfied with their boss.

- **Impact** - This is closely linked to meaning. Part of the narcissistic tendencies of people, everyone wants to think they have impacted the world around them. It is important to communicate the outcomes of activities to the team, so they can see the impact their work has had. This can come in different forms, such as feedback from service users or seeing the end product to which team members contributed.

In addition, it is important to build in reflective reviews at regular intervals with the team to evaluate team dynamics, identify what has gone well, and what could be improved in the coming period. This can be fit around the periodic strategic review, but should be focused on team behaviours and approaches separate from strategic outcomes. While outcomes might be met, there will always be ways the team can develop and grow together to allow for more efficient and effective work.

Motivation mechanisms

There is a great quote (one of many) from Dale Carnegie (2006): "There is only one way under high heaven to get anybody to do anything....And that is by making the other person want to do it." You can best motivate people with the following approach:

- Build initial buy-in for the idea - you can do this by (a) involving the person and/or the team in the initial decision making so they feel ownership of the idea; (b) exploring the idea with the person to identify the personal benefits of the idea; (c) clearly communicating the intended outcomes of the project so the person can see the impact; (d) all of the above.
- Building in regular check-in points around agreed deadlines - it is important to stress that these are check-INs, not check-UPs. The intention is not to judge the person/team on their progress, but to support them in making progress.
- Developmental feedback - as part of the check-ins, help the person/team understand what they are doing well, build their confidence and create positive feedback loops. Help them understand what they can improve, so they do not waste time doing things incorrectly or inefficiently.
- Recognise achievement - this involves having agreed measures of success so the person/team know what they have achieved, when they have achieved it, and the extent to

which they achieved their goal(s). Where good work has been done, recognise it, give credit, and thanks.

While these are quite basic steps, they are very powerful and unfortunately frequently overlooked. Build them into your day-to-day management processes and it will build a motivated, effective, efficient, impactful team.

Managing disagreements

When caught early enough, disagreements can be addressed, mitigated, and potentially resolved. Left unchecked, they will fester. They will grow roots of distrust and misalignment in the team. They will grow into a cancer that can metastasize and spread to other colleagues, so even once you remove the original cause the damage may be far larger and require more drastic action. This is why a trust-based, open-door approach is the most efficient for a CEO. People come to you early with issues. It may seem like your time is being wasted with petty squabbles that arise whenever people work together, but it is worth the time. Be careful to not build a dependency that everything can only be resolved through you. Support the development of your team's emotional intelligence so they can resolve minor issues amongst themselves. But be available as a neutral arbiter and mediator that can be called upon when needed.

Approach the disagreement by collecting the facts from those involved. Preferably separately so it does not become a 'he said, she said' situation. Even when you feel strongly that one side is in the right, listen to all sides. Remember, in a one-on-one disagreement, there are always three sides: one side, the other side, and the truth.

Take a coaching approach as you collect the facts, to help people see where they could have been better as well as hearing how they think the other could have been better. This will help people's emotional reactions to the disagreement as well, supporting them to work through the RULER technique. Defusing the emotional element will always make it easier to resolve the disagreement. Identify the goals and outcomes those involved want from the disagreement. It is likely there will be common ground here. You can then bring everyone together, agree on these central goals and work out a common way forward.

Managing blame and victimisation

A surefire way for a disagreement to escalate into an argument is if the sides start to assign blame and/or victimise. This applies to blaming or victimising themselves, as well as blaming or victimising others. Wayne Dyer compiled an excellent list of blame/victimising statements in his book *Pulling Your Own Strings* (1990), of which you will likely recognise the following common ones:

- I/You/We/They should have... - this statement focuses you on the past and is intended only to make you feel guilty. It limits your ability to learn and grow as it only offers up a hypothetical past where mistakes were not made.
- How could I/you/we/they do that? - like the previous two statements, this question has the underlying assumption that the person knew the outcome before they acted and should have known better. It applies massive guilt but delivers no useful answer.
- If only I/you/we/they had... - same as the 'should have', it is focused on the past rather than consider what could be done in the future if a similar situation is encountered.
- But we've always done it this way... - a fallacious argument from authority, insisting that the past should control the present and future. It always imbues the person suggesting the change with guilt that they are trying to ruin something good.
- If you said it before, why don't you mean it now? - the person is refusing to let the other grow and change their mind, binding them with guilt to the past.
- Whose fault was it? - this limits the mind to assigning blame and then moving on. It prevents anyone from considering multiple factors and elements, from which people could learn and identify constructive ways forward.

Listen out for these statements and others like them. Avoid using them yourself. Constructively challenge someone who uses the statement to ask them to rephrase it in a way that does not simultaneously apply guilt, blame, or victimise.

Managing arguments

It can be challenging to manage arguments. In the moment, you may get caught up in the emotions and just want to make everything okay for everyone. You need to remember to be like a gyroscope - empathetic and moving with the situation, but calm and steady on the inside (O'Neill, 2007). So when a disagreement has escalated into an argument, take a calming breath. Take another few dozen. Practice your RULER technique and with a calm, rational brain approach the argument. Apply the techniques for resolving a disagreement. You may need to reach out for outside support to keep you calm and steady, such as your line manager or coach. That is not a sign of weakness, it is a sign of strength that you recognise you need help.

As a manager and/or CEO, you must remember that you are legally responsible for the workplace and the behaviour of your employees. If something has escalated to an argument, pick up the phone and speak to an HR adviser. There will be very clear legal HR steps you should follow to document the argument, the actions you took, and how this was communicated to all relevant parties. Take meticulous notes. You never know what might escalate into an employment tribunal and you want to be confident that you are not going to be caught out and be liable for thousands of pounds all because you didn't send one critical email. As heartless as that sounds, it is an eventuality you constantly need to mitigate against. Alongside this, care for your team because it is the right thing to do and because you are that type of person. But always make sure legally your back is covered. Because as CEO, from a legal standpoint, you are the organisation first, person second.

Development

One of the most influential things you can do as a CEO to develop your organisation is to develop your people. Helping your people learn and grow will improve efficiency, morale, retention, and attract future top talent. The three main ways to support development are: feedback, training, and coaching. Each builds on the other and each needs to be in place for the largest impact. Regardless of the size of your organisation or your budget, all three can and should be implemented for each member of staff.

Feedback

Feedback should be built into the workday. Continual feedback enables continual learning and improvement. It allows for immediate recognition of positive or negative actions, which allows for immediate learning and/or mitigating actions. Feedback should not be saved up only for formal appraisals or supervisions as you will delay the learning; you will limit the learning (no one is going to sit there for hours as you detail out dozens of comments, you will only select a few to focus on); and you will limit the impact of the learning (the person receiving the feedback will inevitably experience an emotional reaction if they are not used to receiving feedback and therefore they will not be able to fully take on board your comments).

Additionally, saving feedback for formal appraisals and supervisions limits the scope of the feedback from the manager to the direct report. Feedback should be given at all levels, by all employees: by managers to their direct reports, between peers, by direct reports to their managers, and everyone in between. Everyone has the potential to learn and grow, and so everyone should receive feedback. Employees are interdependent and so everyone should have the chance to provide feedback to each other.

With that in mind, not all feedback is useful feedback. Feedback should follow the 4A feedback guidelines (Meyer and Hastings, 2022):

When giving feedback:

AIM TO ASSIST - Feedback must be given with positive intent, to support the individual's development.

ACTIONABLE - Feedback must focus on what the recipient has done well or can do differently.

Example of good feedback: "When you share your ideas in team meetings, you tend to interrupt other members of the team and talk over them. It would be better to let the person finish and then offer a counter-point."

Example of bad feedback: "You are a jerk that never listens."

When receiving feedback:

APPRECIATIVE - When you receive feedback, listen carefully and consider the message with an open mind. Avoid becoming defensive and angry. Show appreciation as the feedback has been given to help you.

ACCEPT OR DISCARD - Both you and the provider of the feedback must understand that the decision to react to the feedback is entirely up to the recipient.

Example of a good reaction to feedback: "Thank you for raising that with me. I had not realised that I was cutting people off in a meeting, and I will focus on listening and waiting for others to finish."

Example of a bad reaction to feedback: "I do not need to listen to your dumb ideas."

In addition, when giving feedback check if the other person is available to receive your comments. They may be experiencing an emotional hijacking (Goleman, 1995) and so they may not be able to process the feedback at that moment. They may be in the middle of a task and cannot be interrupted. For example, if they are in the middle of giving a presentation and you notice that they could better connect with their audience through more eye contact, it's better to wait until after the presentation than to shout it out mid-way. Ask for their consent, for example, "Could I give you some feedback on your presentation now?" and recognise that they may say no. This does not mean that if they say no, you never give feedback. Ask as a follow-up question, "When would be a better time to give you feedback?"

Likewise, when approached by a colleague who would like to give you feedback, take a moment to consider if you are in the right state of mind to receive the feedback. For example, if you have just given a presentation, you might be riding on adrenaline and cannot focus on constructive comments. In which case, set a time in the near future when you will be prepared to receive developmental feedback.

Performance evaluation

Building on this continual feedback, formal performance evaluations, such as appraisals and supervisions, can provide good opportunities to summarise feedback, reflect on common themes, and plan for the future.

Appraisals provide an opportunity for the appraisee and appraiser to:
- Evaluate the appraisee's performance in the previous 6 to 12 months
- Reflect on the appraisee's job satisfaction and identify areas for improvement
- Support the appraisee's professional development
- Set individual strategic targets, based on the organisation's targets, for the subsequent 6 to 12 months.

Appraisals should be conducted every 6 to 12 months for each employee, including you as the CEO. The organisation's Chair or designed Board member should be the appraiser in your appraisal.

Appraisals should be split into four sections: Part A, Part B, Part C, and Part D. The appraisal should be led by the appraiser. It should be conducted in a private professional setting, where the appraisee feels safe to share and receive feedback. The appraiser should guide the appraisee through the questions in the appraisal form and take notes throughout.

Part A should focus on managing expectations for the appraisal to ensure everyone is ready to both give and receive feedback. The basics covered in the Feedback section should be discussed. The appraisee and appraiser should also reflect on what is needed from the role, before evaluating the appraisee's performance. The following statements/questions can prompt effective discussion in Part A:

- I wish my appraiser knew... - Appraisees should use this statement to reflect on any professional or personal matters that they wish their appraiser knew about them. These can be positive or negative, and as detailed as the appraisee wants. For example, "I wish my appraiser knew that I have been working an extra hour a day for the past month to stay on top of my tasks"; "I wish my manager knew that I have been learning Spanish outside of work and I just had my first extended conversation with my Spanish mother-in-law".
- From my job, I need... / I want... - Appraisees should use these statements to articulate their personal wants and needs from the role at the organisation. Asking these questions prompts the appraiser to consider the organisation's responsibility towards the individual.
- From me, the organisation needs... / the organisation wants... - Appraisees should use these statements to reflect on what the organisation needs and wants from their role, in exchange for them receiving their personal needs and wants. Asking these reverse questions prompts the appraisee to consider their obligation to the organisation.
- From this role, the organisation needs... / the organisation wants... - These statements should be answered by the appraiser to reflect back the organisation's actual wants and needs from the appraisee. These questions are designed to clear up any misunderstandings about expectations and to start the appraisal on the same page.

Part B should move on to reflect on the previous 6 to 12 months, to identify what went well, what could have been improved, and what learnings should be taken forward into the next year. The focus is on the appraisee's performance and role. Organisational elements and other members of the team should only be reflected upon in relation to how they impacted the appraisee. Part B should also include a more holistic reflection on the appraisee's role, their job satisfaction, and desired development. The following questions should be considered by both the appraisee and the appraiser:

- How satisfactory has the previous year been for you?

- How have you progressed with your annual targets?
- What went well in the previous year?
- What do you consider to be your most important achievements of the past year and why?
- How could the previous year have been better?
- What challenges, barriers, or bottlenecks did you experience during the previous year? How could these be removed?
- What elements of your role do you find most difficult?
- What elements of your role and work interest you most and least?
- What action could be taken to improve your performance in your current position by you, your line manager, and the rest of the team?
- What do you like and dislike about working for the organisation?
- What kind of role or work would you like to be doing in two years' time?

The appraisee should share their reflections on each question first, with the appraiser adding comments afterwards. This allows for the appraisee to genuinely reflect on each question and take responsibility for their answer, rather than just being told what is good and bad by their appraiser. This will build the appraisee's engagement with the process, which in turn will increase their engagement in development activities.

Part C should focus on 360 feedback from the wider organisation team. Depending on the size of your organisation, it is possible that each employee will need to provide feedback on each employee. For larger organisations, feedback should be collected from 4 to 6 people beyond the appraisee and appraiser, including peers, direct reports, managers, and other relevant stakeholders for the role. When collecting 360 feedback, those providing feedback must be required to state their names, however, the comments should be anonymised in the appraisal. Collecting names means that any troubling comments can be followed up by managers, but presenting them anonymously means the appraisee can focus on the developmental feedback without having professional relationships undermined.

The 360 feedback should involve the appraisee, appraiser, and wider team scoring the appraisee's capability and knowledge in key areas relevant to their role; as well as the appraisee's ability to live the organisational values. Once scored, the appraisee and appraiser should reflect on how the appraisee could improve the scores. The wider team should further be asked to provide comments on the appraisee's strengths; good practise; and areas for improvement. While the appraisee should not be required to integrate all feedback into their practice, the comments should be discussed in turn to identify actionable improvements.

Part D should then focus on the next 6 to 12 months. The appraiser should identify organisational strategic targets relevant to the appraisee's role. The appraisee and appraiser should then distil these into individual strategic targets for the next year, reflecting on what kind of knowledge, skills, and attributes the appraisee will need to fulfil them. If the appraisee is set to become promoted into a management position, it can be useful to review their skills against the leadership pipeline (see section 'What skills do you need as a CEO?') to identify the areas they need to develop. Based on this need, the appraiser and appraisee should discuss the training and support that should be put in place to enable the appraisee to succeed. Finally, the appraisee's job description should be reviewed and updated so it fully reflects the requirements of the appraisee for the next 6 to 12 months.

Following the appraisal, the appraiser should finalise the appraisal notes. Each party should then review the notes and indicate their approval of the record by signing and dating the bottom of the form.

Once all appraisals are complete, you should review all of the appraisal records to:
- Plan training and/or coaching schedules for the subsequent year for each member of the team
- Identify areas for improvement for the organisation to improve job satisfaction
- Apply your compensation policy in response to individual performance.

Training or coaching?

When considering how to address areas for improvement, you will need to decide whether training and/or coaching would be most appropriate. To do this, evaluate two independent variables for the employee and the specific task around which they need to improve (O'Neill, 2007):

1. Their skill and/or competence to do the task
2. Their willingness, confidence, and/or commitment to do the task

Where their skills and/or competence are low, training is appropriate. Where their willingness, confidence, and/or commitment are low, coaching is appropriate.

Training

As stated previously, regardless of the size of your organisation and your budget, all staff should receive training. The training does not need to be expensive, formal, multi-day seminars. There are many different types of training:

- On-the-job training - fellow high performing colleagues can demonstrate different skills and activities, to guide the employee through their tasks. This has no financial cost, although there may be time cost based on how much the person doing the training has to step away from their usual activities.
- Shadowing colleagues - allows an employee to view the behaviours and actions of high performing colleagues in different situations. Shadowing could occur day-to-day (eg. a new receptionist could shadow an existing receptionist for a week during their induction); in specific situations (eg. shadowing a colleague leading a client meeting); and across roles (eg. an intern might shadow different employees across the organisation to get a sense of different roles and how they fit together). If you have good relationships with partner organisations, you may be able to arrange shadowing across organisations as well. While this is a financially cheap option, do consider the cost in terms of decreased efficiency of the person being shadowed.

- Mentoring - a high performing employee could be matched with another employee to talk through their challenges and provide advice and guidance. Similarly to shadowing, this is financially cheap but does incur time costs.
- Massive Open Online Course (MOOC) - many platforms such as FutureLearn and Coursera offer free short virtual courses in key topics that can improve your employees' skills and knowledge. Financially cheap, only takes the time for the individual to complete the course.
- Conferences - this can complement networking and sales activities. Conferences can be a good place to learn more about the sector and 'steal' ideas from similar organisations/competitors. This can be a more expensive option. If you are a non-profit, many conferences offer free or reduced fee tickets.
- Formal training seminars, qualifications, etc - the most time and cost-intensive option. This can be useful when you want to support employees to develop new skills that do not currently exist in the organisation. It is worth vetting these courses as they can cost a lot but deliver little value.

Whichever training solution you select, it is important that prior to the training the employee and their manager collectively agree on the main objectives for the training. Afterwards, you need to build in reflection time between the employee and their manager to identify the extent to which the objectives were met, the key learnings, how they will be integrated into the employee's practice, and further questions or knowledge gaps that may need to be met through other training.

Coaching
Coaching can be incredibly valuable to bring about fundamental personal insights and behaviour changes in employees. A coach creates an environment where the coachee can do their best thinking. The purpose is not to teach but to facilitate learning. It is not structured training where the coachee is told what to do. Coaching is based on the following equation: performance = potential - interference. A coach's role is to help coachee identify their own

interference, mitigate it, unlock their full potential, and improve overall workplace performance.

Coaching can be powerfully delivered within the organisation (e.g. by a manager) and outside of the organisation (e.g. by an external coach). Managers throughout the organisation should be supported to develop their own coaching skills, so they can help bring out the potential of their individual team members. As a CEO, you need to model this behaviour so it can cascade down throughout the organisation.

When coaching, you must remember and embrace the following fundamental tenets (Kline, 1999):

1. You must believe that the coachee has the ability to learn and develop. If you do not believe this, then you will never be able to support the coachee to believe it. If you do not believe this, then what is the point of training them? You must think of the coachee in terms of their potential, not their past performance.
2. As a coach, it is your responsibility to facilitate the thinking of the coachee. The person that should shine in a coaching meeting is the coachee. It is not a time to score points or seem impressive as the coach.
3. Avoid hiding your opinion in a question. Questions should be used to help a coachee explore the issue, the situation, their options, and/or their next steps. If you have an opinion, ask the coachee if they are receptive to hearing it and then share it openly.
4. You need to be emotionally neutral towards the coachee and the people that they speak about.
5. Avoid blame and judgement. Once someone or something is blamed, the need to explore reasons behind outcomes and mitigating actions for the future is cut off. Judgement puts people on the defensive, which limits their capacity to think.
6. The quality of your attention determines the quality of the coachee's thinking. Do not think about what you'll say next or what you think they should do. During your coaching sessions, focus solely on them.
7. Avoid "drive-by questioning" (Bungay Stanier, 2016) where you riddle someone with a series of questions. Rather than

feeling supportive, it will feel like an interrogation. Ask one question at a time.

When you are coaching, your aim is to build your coachee's awareness and sense of responsibility for themselves. In coaching sessions, the (T)GROW Model can be used to structure the coachee's thinking (Whitmore, 2017):

- (T) - Topic - what does the coachee want to discuss?
- G - Goal - what do they want to achieve? What outcome would they like from the coaching conversation?
- R - Reality - what is the current situation? What are the challenges?
- O - Options - how could the coachee bridge from their current situation to their goal?
- W - Way - what will they do? By when? How will they know they were successful?

During your coaching sessions, the following techniques can be useful:

- WAIT (Bungay Stanier, 2016) - Why Am I Talking? - Embrace silence in sessions, as this can be when coachees do their best thinking. Do not rush to fill the silence. Stay focused, give the coachee supportive attention, and wait. Repeat your question to see if there are any more insights. Only when the coachee settles that there is nothing else to say, then move on.
- Model T (Downey, 2014) - when exploring the 'reality' and 'options', follow the broad top of the 'T' to explore the breadth of the situation. Then focus in on the long tail of the 'T' to explore each sub-issue in depth to identify the 'ways' forward.
- AWE (Bungay Stanier, 2016) - And What Else? - give the person space to keep thinking and explore other facets of the issue.
- Constructive challenging - be open to challenging the coachee's limiting assumptions or discrepancies. Remember to do this without judgment - the focus is helping their development, not point-scoring. When setting up a new coaching relationship, it is a good idea to establish how such challenging can supportively be communicated.

Integrating coaching sessions into line management one-to-one meetings can be especially effective. It can build a sense of responsibility within an employee, allowing them to internalise the fact that they are in control of their own actions and have the power to bring about change. This should encourage employees to think through issues more broadly and generate possible solutions, rather than just relying on their manager to solve every problem. As a manager, it allows you to provide effective support, even in areas in which you are not an expert.

Managing crises

For all of your planning, preparation, and precaution, things will go wrong. Everyone's tolerance for things going wrong will vary, but it turns into a crisis when it feels threatening, unstable, and unpredictable. Crises can emerge from within an organisation and/or from external circumstances. A major funder may not deliver on their commitment and your income streams may dry up to the point that you cannot pay your team. A disagreement between colleagues may fester to the point that it divides the team and turns them against one another. A global pandemic may hit and the entire world is shut down for an unknowable amount of time. You will face crises as a CEO, and you will be expected to deal with them. There may be some that cannot be solved, but their impact can be lessened and the damage dampened.

The following steps provide a structure for how to approach a crisis. Depending on the crisis you face, these steps may need to be taken within a few minutes, across several hours, or even across several days. Focus on doing the best you can with the time you have. If you can only spend two minutes per step, then look to maximise those two minutes.

The first step is to stop panicking. It is okay to feel out of your depth. It is okay to feel afraid. It is okay to not know how you'll get through. But you need to stop panicking. Take a breath and calm yourself. As the CEO, you will need to lead your team through the crisis. You will need to be strong for them.

The second step is to gather as much information as possible about the situation you are in. Gathering information buys you mental space to calm down, think, and strategise. This may require you to ask questions of team members, review internal reports, read external reviews, and watch the news. There will always be unknown unknowns - things that cannot ever be known. But you want to reduce the number of known unknowns - gaps you are aware that exist in your knowledge. In gathering information, you should look to get a workable level of knowledge to understand the basic causes of the crisis, draft scenarios of how the crisis will impact your organisation, and the extent of the anticipated damage.

When you feel you have enough of a grasp of the situation to be able to comprehensively explain it to someone else, you need to bring it to the attention of others. Who those 'others' are will depend on your specific situation - it could be colleagues, the whole team, your governing body, your regulators, and national watchdogs. You will need to calmly explain the situation and your assessment of the impact of the crisis. Clear communication is key. If people believe you are being honest with them, they will be more inclined to listen and work with you. If they think you are hiding things, then they will be suspicious and likely assume the worst (both about you and the crisis). Do not feel under pressure to have all the answers at this point. Be honest about what you know and what you do not know. Be sensitive to the fact that the news will not be welcome and people will likely respond emotionally. Do not ignore the emotion, but do not be consumed by it. Recognise the emotional response and then channel it into finding a way forward through the crisis.

Depending on the situation, this can be a good moment to open up a discussion about how the crisis could be mitigated. Make it clear that the final decision will rest with you (or another designated authority e.g. your governing body or regulator), but that you welcome input so you can think through all facets of the crisis. Make it clear how much time you have to listen to suggestions, recognising the time pressures that often come with crises. Giving people a voice and listening to them gives people a small sense of control among the chaos and builds their engagement around identifying solutions. If people start to complain, you should respond firmly by stating that concerns and complaints will be heard after the immediate crisis is averted, but the focus for the moment should be on finding a way forward. Concerns and complaints are only useful if they identify a shortcoming in the proposed plan, and they should be accompanied by an idea for an alternative approach.

When you have collected the suggestions, you will then need to formulate a plan. This could be done within the meeting or individually by yourself afterwards. Whatever helps you think clearly and objectively will be the best option for you. You may only have a skeleton of a plan, just the next steps to take as the crisis starts to unfold. For example, in the case of a global pandemic, it may just be how to keep the lights on for a few weeks until the government announces their next plan.

When your plan is authorised (by you, your governing body, your regulator, etc), then you need to once again communicate it clearly and firmly to your team. State the facts and make it clear if the time for input has passed. Provide regular updates so people do not start to confabulate and fill in the gaps. Even if the update is that you do not know anything new, let them know as this will build trust that you will tell them when there is something to tell.

Throughout all of the above steps, you should continue to gather as much information as possible to refine your plans further as you become better aware of the situation, the possible scenarios for your organisation, and the anticipated damage. You should define clear times where input from others is welcome, as it is always beneficial to have multiple perspectives on a problem, even if it only highlights what you cannot do. In undertaking these consultations, again, you need to be firm that input can be given but the final decisions will be made by you (or another designated authority). During a crisis, having a very clear chain of command gives people a sense of structure, which reduces the mental impact of chaos. This gathering of information will then trigger repeated mini strategic planning sessions as you cycle through your market analyses, consultations, SWOT analyses, strategic plans, operational plans, and resources plans.

Revisiting your strategic, operational, and resources plans will be key if the crisis has the potential to shut down your organisation. As a crisis unfolds, you will be able to start estimating the anticipated amount of time it will take to implement your mitigating plans. You can then review your business-as-usual strategic and operational plans to identify what work needs to be put on hold to free up time to manage the crisis. As a small organisation, you will likely be operating at 100% capacity so there will definitely be things that have to be paused, stopped, or cancelled to manage a crisis. You can then manage expectations within your team, with your governing body, with your partners, etc about when they can anticipate planned work will actually take place.

Reviewing your resources plan will also mean you can identify where tough decisions need to be made so the organisation can weather the storm. Translating your plans into financial terms, you will be able to see to what extent you need to secure new income sources, cut costs, and/or restructure. It is rare in a crisis that you have to immediately jump to making people redundant, but if it does become clear that you need to let people go, then giving as much advance notice as possible is not only the right thing to do, it is legally mandated. For the UK, ACAS provides a free step-by-step guide on how to approach redundancies.

It is important to remember that crises are not inherently bad. Continually assessing information and rethinking the situation will help you identify where crises can be turned into opportunities. It can help you identify more efficient and effective ways of working as you adapt to the crisis. It can highlight weak points in the organisation that can be addressed, which builds the organisation's resilience in case of recurrent crises. It can identify new sectors and/or new audiences to which the organisation can pivot. At the very least, a crisis can be a learning opportunity for you to develop as a CEO. It will inform your experience and allow you to face the next crisis with a bit more confidence and calmness as you can look back on what you have already endured.

PART 3

OPERATIONS

Finance

As the CEO of a small organisation, it is unlikely that you will have a Chief Financial Officer or even a bookkeeper as part of your team. You may have an administrative officer, who looks after receipts and logs transactions on a piece of software. However, all financial decision making, authorisation, and reporting will ultimately be your responsibility, including:

- Income
- Expenditure
- Banking
- Payroll
- Pensions
- Financial reporting
- Annual accounts and audit

When you join a new organisation, one of your operational priorities will be to understand the finances and financial procedures. You need to know the procedures for all of the listed areas, as well as the authorisation requirements and involved persons for each.

Income

The main question you need to consider at all times is: do you have enough income to support your intended expenditure (and meet the profit expectations of your shareholders if you are in the for-profit sector)? This question will always be front and centre with every decision you make as a CEO as every decision has a financial implication. If the answer is yes, then a main source of stress that plagues CEOs is lessened. If the answer is no, then you need to re-evaluate your strategy, and your budget, and prioritise better. Of course, the answer to the question is always time-dependent. You will always need to consider your income sources and ensure you have sufficient to cover your intended expenditure as you move forward.

In addition to that main question, you will need to work through the following questions when you are new to an organisation, and it is information you should always have at the back of your mind as part of your decision making.

What are your key sources of income? Do you have one main source, a few main sources, or lots of little sources? Are they interdependent or independent? How reliable are your income sources? It is always recommended that you have a diverse portfolio of income sources, but you should take this advice with a pinch of salt. If you have one or two highly reliable sources of income, then looking to diversify may reduce your ability to deliver the product(s) / service(s) that generates that income and you may undermine the reliability of the income sources. Having few sources of income can mean you need less staff time to generate the income; you can better monitor risk and reliability; and you can build a strong relationship with the income sources. It can also mean you are exposed and vulnerable if something happens to those income sources. Therefore, there is no 'correct' number of income sources, it is something you need to work out for your own organisation.

Who is involved in securing the income sources? This will include the person(s) responsible for sales/fundraising/marketing; the person(s) responsible for creating the product / delivering the service; and also the administrative staff involved in invoicing and processing income. Are all the individuals involved aware of their roles and how they interlink in terms of income generation? This can be a key point where you can improve income generation and efficiency in a small organisation. Organisations that have grown organically and have a small team may have several people wearing different hats who are not entirely sure how they fit together. There may be redundancies, unintended time wasting, and confusion which can be cleared up by clearly defining roles and responsibilities. You want to make sure income generation is as smooth and efficient as possible, as it is one of the main areas where the adage "time is money" applies.

What is the pipeline for your income generation? What are the steps involved? What is the timeline? Do you receive your income for the year in one lump sum or is it spaced out over the year? This will determine your cash flow, which in turn will impact your expenditure. If you receive all of your income in lump sums, then you need to adequately budget out expenditure so you do not run out of cash to pay for essential expenditure (e.g. payroll) between the lumps. If income flows in small amounts continuously, then you need to

115

budget to save for larger expenses during the year or secure a credit line/overdraft from your bank. If your income is unreliable and unpredictable, then you will need to be much more conservative with expenditure to avoid running out of cash.

If you are in the fortunate position of generating a surplus/profit, then you need to consider what is done with excess income. Do you have a required level of reserves (e.g. your regulator requires you to have at least 12 months of operating expenditure as reserves to protect your service users)? Can you invest the surplus to create a new source of longer-term income? Can you pump the surplus back into the organisation e.g. into additional staff, additional resources, additional services? Does your organisation's legal structure require you to issue dividend payments or profit share? While you might have a surplus this year, what does next year look like? If you anticipate a deficit the following year, it is worth holding the reserves to balance out the books. More on financial forecasting below.

Expenditure

Alongside income, you will need to keep a close eye on expenditure. A central question to have in your head with all expenditure is: "Is this necessary?" Again, you would be surprised at the level of savings an organisation can achieve with that question. Even when an expense is necessary, asking if the level of expense is necessary can prompt you to find a cheaper alternative or even assure you that the expense is worth a premium cost. For example, when fitting out a new office, an air conditioning system may seem like an extravagant expense. But then considering the benefit to staff morale and productivity during extreme summer heat, you may realise the system will pay for itself over the course of a summer where staff can actually get on with their jobs. Or you may realise that the benefit is necessary, but there are alternative ways to achieve the outcome. In any case, pausing and considering expenses will reduce the likelihood of waste. And in a small organisation, where income may not be as large as desired, ensuring you only spend on necessary things may mean the difference between survival and folding.

It can be helpful to think about your 'return on investment' with expenditure. What can you expect in return for the expenditure? For example, if you spend £100 on marketing materials, which then results in £1000 worth of net income then your return on investment is 900% (£1000-£100/£100 * 100). Return on investment can be a useful way to consider how necessary and beneficial certain expenses can be. However, it does rely on you turning every benefit into a financial figure, which can be difficult with intangible things like staff morale. You can only use a proxy figure, such as staff productivity represented by staff working hours, which may not be fully accurate. Therefore, always be cautious with financial approximations - do not let the numbers become more meaningful than the non-financial value and benefit you may be creating.

Similar to income, you will need to consider the following for expenditure in addition to that central question.

What are your main streams of expenditure? Are they interdependent or independent? Are there any efficiencies that can be achieved to cut costs long term? For example, high electricity bills could be reduced long term through a short term larger expenses such as installing photovoltaics or buying more energy-efficient machinery.

Who is involved in expenditure? What are your processes for authorising expenditure? What are your processes for monitoring expenditure? You need to make sure that every member of the team knows how much they can spend without authorisation; what expenses can be claimed for reimbursement; how they will be reimbursed; who can authorise larger expenses; and how to evidence expenses.

You should not be afraid of spending money. However, you should always be cautious and considerate in your expenditure. The organisation relies on you to ensure its continued existence. Your team relies on you for their monthly pay. You rely on you for your monthly pay. Pay for what is necessary, but no more. Of course, as CEO, it is up to you to decide the definition of necessary for your organisation. Do not squander your resources.

A note: as CEO, you will experience a conflict of interest any time you authorise an item of expenditure for your own benefit. For example, purchasing a new work laptop for your use. It can be a slippery slope as you can easily justify a more extravagant purchase with the claim that it will enable you to work better and so it will ultimately benefit the organisation. If you are very conscientious, you may slip the other way as you do not want to abuse your position by buying things for yourself. In either case, consider whether you would authorise the expenditure for a different member of the team. It can help to think about the person you least like on your team (not that CEOs ever dislike team members...). If you would authorise the expense for them, then it is safe to do so for yourself without it being an abuse of power. If not, then re-evaluate whether the purchase is necessary (or whether your dislike of the team member gets in the way of authorising necessary expenses for them).

Banking

A few basics you need to know:
- How many bank accounts do you have?
- How do you access each bank account? Who else has the ability to access the bank accounts?
- How much overall cash do you have? How is this distributed between bank accounts? Are your accounts covered under the Financial Services Compensation Scheme (FSCS), which protects up to £85,000 per bank account?
- If you have investments and/or assets, how is their liquidity managed? How easily can they be converted to cash should you need it?
- How do you receive bank statements? Who reviews bank accounts and reconciles bank statements? What oversight is there of that person?
- How is the state of your bank accounts reported to you as CEO?
- How does your organisation meet your banks' compliance and anti-fraud requirements? How do you manage large payments, so that your bank does not block the payment or even freeze your account?
- How were the banks chosen? What are the banking fees?

It is important that as the CEO, you regularly review your financial statements to mitigate against fraud. While it is important to trust your team, you do need to verify that trust and make sure that any dodgy dealings can be caught as soon as possible. It is easy to fudge numbers on a budget spreadsheet, but you cannot get around the actual bank statements.

Payroll

If you have an employee, then you will need to have payroll. Payroll is a highly specialised field, which involves a lot of dealings with HMRC and should not be underestimated. It is worth having a trained specialist. In a small organisation, it can be useful (and cheaper) to outsource this job to an external company.

In setting up a contract with an external payroll company, you will need to determine the following:

- What is their overall fee and how is it calculated? Some companies charge a base fee and then an additional fee per staff member. Some companies have tiered fees, where they have a fee linked to overall staff numbers. Some companies just have an overall fee. This is important to find out, especially if you are considering growing as the cheapest option now may quickly become the most expensive one with a few new hires.
- What is included in their fee? Do they calculate the payroll only? Do they oversee the transfers of payment to the employees? Do they send out payslips? Do they calculate pension contributions? Do they oversee the payment of pension contributions? Do they submit the required annual forms to HMRC? If you want a full service, you will need to arrange all of the above with the payroll company. The more you can agree for them to do, the less you will need to worry about getting wrong on a monthly basis.
- What platforms do they use? What time of the month do they calculate payroll? When do you need to authorise payments? You will want to review all payroll calculations prior to authorising payments. Mistakes are sometimes made and it is a real headache to deal with after employees have been under/overpaid. It can be helpful to have a spreadsheet for yourself, in which you have a breakdown of each employee's daily pay, which can then be multiplied by the days worked

that month. You can then compare your figures against the payroll company's calculations. If you have a fairly stable payroll from one month to the next, you can always compare against the previous months' figures to review if they are consistent.

The following things will need to be calculated and paid through payroll:

- Employee(s) salary: the company pays this at the contractually agreed frequency (e.g. weekly, monthly).
- Employee(s) pre-tax benefits: you may have a package of benefits for staff such as the cycle scheme, childcare vouchers, and pensions. The cost of these is deducted from an employee's salary prior to being taxed. This does not equal a saving for you as the company, it just means that part of the overall amount you would pay an employee instead goes somewhere else. HMRC has an excellent guide on staff expenses and benefits. It is worth reviewing this whenever you offer a benefit as they have different tax requirements.
- Employee(s) national insurance: as the company, you will pay a percentage per employee. This is in addition to the employee's salary and is an additional cost to the company. A proportion of the employee's salary will also be deducted as the employee's contribution to national insurance.
- Employee(s) tax: this is deducted from the employee's salary and does not result in an additional cost to the company.
- Employee(s) student loans: this is deducted from the employee's salary and does not result in an additional cost to the company.
- Pension contribution: there will be an employer's contribution which will result in an additional cost to the company. There will be an employee's contribution which is deducted from their overall salary. More on this below.

Once all of those calculations have been made, you will be left with the salary actually sent to the employee (with their tax, national insurance, benefits, student loans, pension contributions deducted); an amount to be sent to HMRC (including the employer's national insurance, the employee's tax, employee's national insurance, employee's student loans); an amount to send to the pension

120

provider (including the employer's contribution and the employee's contribution); and potentially an amount to send to the company that provides your employee benefits. It can be quite complex to work out how much needs to be sent where, which is why it is so beneficial to have a specialist do the calculations for you. It is even better if they complete all the paperwork and actually make the payments on your behalf.

Pensions

If you have a good payroll company that calculates your pension requirements, then you have won half the battle.

In the UK, all employers must offer a workplace pension scheme by law. All staff that earn above a certain threshold must be automatically enrolled on the pension scheme - however, they have the right to opt out. If an employee opts out of the pension scheme, they must be consulted every three years at a minimum to check if they would like to re-enrol. They should be allowed to re-enrol at any time. The HMRC has a clear website that explains all of the requirements.

As a legal minimum, an employer must pay 3% of an employee's salary into the pension scheme, and the employee must pay 5% of their salary into the pension scheme. From a company's point of view, this means that you must pay the employee's full salary; the employer's national insurance contribution (usually 13.8%); and the employer's pension contribution (minimum 3%). This can mean that you pay a total of 16.8% of an employee's salary IN ADDITION to their salary on a monthly basis. These are significant and often forgotten costs of payroll and this should be considered when you are deciding on new employees' salaries. You will always be paying significantly more than the person receives as their take-home pay.

As CEO, you will need to identify a pension company that will operate your organisation's pension pot. Pensions are usually invested by the pension company, to help grow the pension pot ahead of employees' retirement. Because of this investment, all pensions have inherent risk because any investment can lose money as well as make money. Therefore, it is worthwhile picking a larger pension company that oversees many pensions to reduce the likelihood it will run out of money and go bankrupt during financial downturns. Other factors that you could consider in picking a pension company are:

- The pension company fees - all companies will charge you for the benefit of looking after the pensions, in addition to the pension contributions you are paying in. This is another cost on top of all the other payroll costs already listed above.
- Pension contribution requirements - local authority pension companies and some private pension companies set a higher rate of employer contribution to compensate for deficits in the pension pot. If you do not have control over this, you may end up paying very high pension contributions and deficit payments over and above the legal minimum. Again, this can be very costly.
- The pension company reporting - each pension company will require you to share pension contribution details on a monthly basis, however, they will all have their own methods for collecting this information. For some, it is a smooth monthly upload through a modern online portal; for others, it is a convoluted spreadsheet and annual manual report. It can be very time consuming and it is worth considering prior to commitment.
- The level of control individual employees have over their own pension pots - can they set the risk levels? Do they have access to an online portal in which they can monitor their pension investment? Are there ethical investment options available?

Pensions seem very straightforward, but there are many possible hidden costs and time-consuming elements. It is worth reviewing your options carefully before you select a company. If you inherit a pension company when you join as a new CEO, it is worthwhile reviewing the arrangements and identifying if alternatives would be better. It may save you a significant headache every month.

Financial reporting
You will need to bring all of the above together into a budget for the organisation. Your budget should be split into two main sections: income; and expenditure. In a spreadsheet, list out all of the main

sources of your income, followed by all of your main streams of expenditure. Total each section and subtract your expenditure from your income. This is referred to as a profit and loss statement or P&L statement.

For your organisation, you will need to monitor ongoing income and expenditure; and also forecast it ahead. This should be done at regular time intervals that are meaningful to your organisation, usually linked to the time intervals in your strategic plan e.g. monthly, quarterly, annually.

In forecasting a budget, start with your income sources. Consider the information you have available and make an educated estimate of the income you anticipate you will be able to generate. Always take a conservative view: it is better to underestimate your income than to overestimate it. By underestimating, you can review and adjust your spending during the year. By overestimating, you may spend too much and run out of money.

Once you know how much you anticipate you will earn, move on to estimating expenditure. Look to your previous expenditure levels as a base for estimating for the next time interval. Always adjust the overall expenditure estimates for inflation. In the UK, the Consumer Prices Index including owner occupiers' housing costs (CPIH) is a good index on which to base your inflation costs. The full list of expenditure will vary for each organisation, but the following 'overhead' expenses are likely to be included:
- Salaries, national insurance, pensions
- Staff training budget
- Staff travel and expenses
- Premises costs (including rent, utilities, business rates)
- Insurance
- Office supplies and postage
- Telephones
- IT (including website, databases, software licenses, equipment)
- Professional fees (such as accountants, legal advisors, payroll and pensions consultancies, HR consultancies)

It is impossible to know for certain what your income and expenditure will be. Therefore, you will be basing your estimations on assumptions of what might happen in the future. You should record these assumptions as footnotes alongside the budget forecast so that they can be reviewed and adjusted as more information becomes available.

Once you have a budget forecast, you will need to monitor actual income and expenditure alongside it. This allows you to both see how you are doing alongside your estimations, and also better judge the accuracy of your estimation to inform your future forecasting.

Annual accounts and audit

At least once a year, you will need to have an accountant review your financial information to compile your annual accounts. The dates of your financial year will depend on when your organisation was set up. The UK tax year runs from 6 April until the following 5 April, and many organisations time their accounts around this time period. However, some link it to the calendar year, while others link it to different significant events relevant to their business (for example, educational organisations tend to follow the academic year of 1 August to 31 July). Regardless of the timing, once a year you will need to produce annual accounts. If you are a registered company, you will need to submit the annual accounts to Companies House. You will also need to file a Confirmation Statement on an annual basis. As a registered charity, you may need to submit it to Companies House as well as the Charity Commission.

Like with payroll, producing annual accounts and properly submitting the relevant information to your relevant financial regulator can be highly technical and it is recommended that you use a trained accountant for the job. They will require all of your financial information for the year, including:
- Bank account statements
- Access to your financial monitoring systems (e.g. spreadsheets, cloud-based software)
- Financial records (such as payroll calculations, receipts, invoices)

- Governance minutes (e.g. minutes from Directors' meetings/trustee meetings)

Alongside this information, they will ask for a Directors'/Trustees' report to summarise the previous year. Depending on the legal structure of your organisation, you will be required to include different levels of information for regulatory review. Charities especially need to produce a lengthy report evidencing how they have delivered public benefit through their aims and objectives in the previous year.

In reviewing the financial information, the accountant will be required to judge whether they think your organisation has sufficient resources available to continue operating for another financial year. This is referred to as the "going concern" and you want to be deemed as a going concern.

Depending on your organisational size and regulatory requirements, you may also need to undergo an audit alongside your annual accounts. While your annual accounts could be compiled by an accountant employed by your organisation, the audit should be undertaken by an external auditor. The purpose of an audit is to inspect your annual accounts to determine their accuracy and compliance. Auditors will review the same information as the accountant, and they will 'test' the information by asking for all evidence related to randomly selected financial transactions. They will also require that all Directors / Trustees and key staff complete related parties' forms identify any conflicts of interest which could indicate fraudulent activities. The audit will likely involve a lengthy meeting with the audit team in which they ask questions about the financial year, to clarify any uncertainty they may have, and further test the information they have been provided. It can be an intimidating meeting, but it is important to stay calm and answer fully and truthfully. They will not be trying to trip you up, there will be no trick questions. If you do not understand a technical term, ask them to explain what they mean, as this will allow you to answer their questions accurately.

At the end of the audit, you will receive the audit report, which will include a list of any concerning activities the audit uncovered and a list of recommendations on how financial procedures and practices could be improved in the future. The concerns should be addressed immediately, and the recommendations should be implemented as far as possible as it will increase the financial security of your organisation against fraud and/or malpractice.

Compliance

An organisation exists as a legal entity, and there is a wide range of laws and regulations that govern what an organisation can and cannot do. Different organisational structures will have additional specialist regulations, such as charities and voluntary groups. As a CEO, you need to be aware of the different rules as ignorance is no defence if you break them. Common sense goes a long way in keeping you compliant, but you do need to research and keep yourself updated.

As with financial matters, it is prudent to secure legal advice for your organisation regardless of your size. There are many legal consultancies that exist that specialise in supporting small organisations and have tiered fees depending on organisational size. Some offer a standard monthly fee, while others charge based on usage. You will need to consider the different legal areas you may need support and then decide on which option will give you the most support while being the most cost-effective.

Governance

All organisations will have a highest governing authority that sits above the CEO to provide oversight and serve as the legally responsible representatives of the organisation. You will have a legal document, such as articles of association or a constitution, that sets out the legal purpose of your organisation, the responsibilities of your highest governing authority, and the legal requirements that the highest governing authority must follow. This will usually include: how meetings are called; frequency of meetings; how resolutions are made; how representatives are elected; and how representatives step down.

With your highest governing authority, you will want to ensure you have a broad range of skills and experiences that are relevant to your organisation. The skills/experience that will be common across organisations are:

- Legal - who can advise on legal matters such as HR, contracting, data protection

- Finance - who can act as the organisation's treasurer and support you with budgeting and accounting
- Income generation - relevant to your income generation types such as business-to-customer sales, membership growth, grant fundraising
- Communications - who can support you in sharing your organisation's story and products/services
- Lived sector experience - who represents your customers/beneficiaries and can give you insight into the benefits/shortcomings of your ideas

It is worthwhile creating a skills register in which you identify all of the skills and experience you need for your organisation. You can then review which governing members address which needs. Where gaps exist, you can then target those gaps with recruitment.

Alongside skills and experience, you should consider how representative your board is of the community you wish to serve. A mix of life experiences, backgrounds, cultures, ethnicities, ages, gender identities, sexual orientations, religions, and physical and mental abilities will enrich your ideas and implementation. What is important when recruiting anyone, but especially when you are recruiting a diverse group of people, is that they all abide by the organisation's values and they believe in the organisation's purpose and mission. People are united with a common goal and agreed approach.

Your governing body will need a Chair and a Vice Chair to lead them. Your legal articles of association/constitution should define how these posts are elected and the term of the posts. These are not empty, figure-head roles. The Chair and Vice Chair can have an enormously beneficial or disastrously detrimental impact on your organisation. As previously mentioned, they must abide by the organisation's values and believe in the mission. They should lead from the front on this and be role models for the other governing body representatives. They should not be selected only because they have the time or they are ambitiously building their CV. Like you as the CEO, they must be able to lead and manage a team. They must be able to run meetings and facilitate discussions. They must be able to manage conflicts and garner support for actions. They must follow through and stick to commitments. They must be able to line manage, as they are likely going to line manage you as CEO.

As CEO, you should make sure there are clear role descriptions for your Chair and Vice Chair, so they know the full commitment they are undertaking. Your governing body is an extension of your team and you should be actively involved in shaping it. Of course, the governing body will sit above you in authority, so you can only make suggestions. But having well-reasoned arguments will go a long way in getting you the support you need. And by support, do not interpret this as a board of yes-men who approve anything you put in front of them. Support means a board who will engage in discussion, who constructively challenge you, who provide oversight so you do not diverge from the strategy or abuse your position, and who are there for you with guidance and advice. As the common saying goes, it is lonely at the top. A strong and effective board makes it less lonely.

Committees

Sitting underneath your highest governing body, you may find it beneficial to create committees. Committees can consist of representatives from your governing body or other external individuals, who can advise on specialised matters. For example, a health charity may have a Patient Committee with different patients that represent the condition the charity is looking to support, who can advise on the patient's perspective and experience. They may also have a Scientific Advisory Committee with different medical and research experts who can advise on different projects the charity might support to address issues raised by the Patient Committee.

With any committee you establish, communicate expectations, authority, and commitment clearly at the outset. This is usually captured within a Terms of Reference, in which you identify the purpose of the committee, the membership, frequency of meeting, set agenda items, modes of communication, decision making authority, and reporting. As with the governing body, make sure that whomever you appoint to the committees is committed to your organisational purpose and values. Someone can be an expert in the area where you need guidance, but that does not inherently make them right to sit on your committee.

Committees can also be valuable opportunities to develop the meeting skills of your governing body representatives, especially your Vice Chair. Your Vice Chair can learn how to run effective committee meetings where the stakes are not as high as governing body meetings. It also provides a separate space for you and your Vice Chair to work together, which can strengthen your professional relationship and bond. This will serve you both well when they take on the mantle of Chair.

Agendas

When you have a meeting in which decisions have to be made, an agenda is an indispensable tool. It sets out clear intentions for the purpose of the meeting, which will help keep participants focused and prevent things from being forgotten or skipped. A good Chair will use the agenda to provide structure and guide timekeeping. A good agenda is supported by good discussion papers. Anywhere where prior knowledge is required, a paper should be provided so that participants can prepare and make informed decisions in the meeting.

For governing body meetings, the agenda will likely be quite long as there will be set items (such as budget review, risk review, strategic progress updates) and new items (such as new partnership opportunities, reports from regulators). It can be useful to categorise agenda items into three sections: (a) items for discussion, (b) items for approval where discussion is not expected, and (c) items for report. This allows the governing body to give adequate time for key discussion items and then more swiftly run through items for sign off and reference. As CEO, it is likely you will draft the agenda and associated papers. You should then arrange to discuss the agenda with your Chair so that they can sign off the categorisation of the agenda items, request additional information, and add their own agenda items.

Agendas and associated papers should be sent out at least one week prior to a meeting, preferably two weeks, to provide adequate time for preparation. Meeting participants should be allowed the opportunity to add agenda items as well during that time and make requests to move items up from category (b) and (c) into category (a) if they feel it warrants more discussion.

Minutes

All governing body meetings must have formal minutes. At a minimum, meeting minutes should record who was present at the meeting, what were the agenda items discussed, and what actions were agreed with set deadlines and assigned responsibilities. Beyond this, you may find it useful to capture the general discussion around each agenda item for your future reference should similar issues arise in future. It can also serve as a useful summary for any governing body representatives unable to attend a meeting. Minutes should be reviewed by all present and collectively agreed to be an accurate summary of the meeting before they are officially filed. Each organisation will have a different length of time minutes have to be kept, mandated by their regulators. In general, a minimum of 10 years is a good rule of thumb. However, in the digital age, it is difficult to argue for a reason to dispose of minutes as they serve as a form of institutional memory and you can learn a lot from reviewing previous minutes.

Human resources

How to manage your 'human resources' (aka your team) and build an effective team has already been covered in the Management section in Part 2. That section (and hopefully this entire field guide) has made the case that you should treat your team members well and consider their needs as people, beyond just employees from which to extract value. This section, therefore, focuses purely on your statutory duties towards your human resources and the policies you need to have in place to cover your organisation's behind.

In the UK, ACAS provides excellent free resources on all things to do with human resources (HR). They provide overviews on what each legal requirement is, the different ways in which an employer can fulfil those requirements, and even have template policies and letters to use. If you cannot afford specialist advice from an HR consultant or your own HR manager, then the ACAS website should be bookmarked and consulted whenever dealing with team issues.

Like with any legal requirements, your HR policies and procedures are not 'nice to haves'. They are mandatory. Ignorance is no defence - even if you are not aware that there is a legal requirement in place, you will be expected to abide by it. The baseline legal requirements are the same for any size of organisation that has employees (this can include volunteers). There then may be further requirements on larger organisations, such as reporting on gender pay gaps and monitoring modern slavery.

As of July 2017 in the UK, employment tribunal fees were abolished as they were deemed unlawful. As a result, an employee can take their employer to employment tribunal court without incurring any costs beyond their own legal fees. If they are successful in their claim, the employer will often be required to pay the legal fees of their employee as well as all the compensation awarded by the courts. It should be noted that this is a fair and correct change as people should not be kept from seeking justice by high legal fees.

Because of this change, there has been a significant increase in the number of cases being taken to tribunal. There has also been a swell in the number of "no win-no fee" solicitors who will only charge when they win a case for an employee. Again, this is a positive development in protecting individuals from abuse as it lowers the barrier to seeking justice. However, it has resulted in a few taking an opportunistic approach to justice. A disgruntled employee could go to a solicitor and together trawl through all of your HR policies and procedures with a fine-tooth comb to find anything that is non-compliant and then push for legal action. Compensation awards tend to be in the tens of thousands in addition to the legal fees, so it can significantly impact a small organisation's financial position.

Therefore, pay attention to HR. Treat employment tribunals as a potentially serious risk to your organisation and put in place the actions to mitigate the risk. Keep your policies up to date. If you can afford it, there are many HR consultant companies that exist, which will provide telephone/email/face-to-face guidance with any HR queries and concerns that you may have. These companies tend to scale their fees based on the size of your organisation, so it can be quite affordable. They often provide insurance for you as part of this, which pays out tribunal compensation awards on your behalf if you can demonstrate that you followed their advice at each stage leading up to the tribunal. If you cannot afford an external consultancy, check to see if they have a newsletter available. Most companies will offer a monthly newsletter and free HR webinars that will give you basic updates on HR legislation changes. By attending these, you will be aware of what the new requirements are and you can amend your policies and procedures accordingly.

Tribunals

If you do have the misfortune of having an employee threaten legal action, then you will likely go through the following steps:

1. The employee should be supported to go through your internal processes for raising a grievance. Depending on the seriousness of their grievance, it is possible it could be dealt with informally or it may need formal review. This will include them submitting their grievance in writing, you investigating by reviewing relevant evidence and speaking with them (and any other employees that are related to the issue).

2. If the issue is not resolved, you could consider mediation using an independent and impartial person to find an acceptable solution.

3. If the issue still is not resolved, then the employee needs to inform ACAS that they want to make a claim to an employment tribunal. ACAS will then support the employee (the "claimant") and your organisation (the "respondent") through early conciliation to try and resolve the issue. You can contact ACAS on behalf of the organisation to request early conciliation as well.

4. If the issue still is not resolved, then the employee will file their claim with the employment tribunal court in which they will state all of the issues they wish to be considered. The period of time they have to make their claim from the point of the issue is limited, usually to between 3-6 months depending on the issue.

5. Once the claim has been received, you will have up to 28 days to respond to the claim detailing your side of the issue. It is crucial you get legal assistance in responding so that all the matters of the case can clearly be presented at this point. The tribunal will then decide whether the case will be heard in court or whether they can make a decision at this stage.

6. If a hearing is to go ahead, you and the employee may be invited to a preliminary hearing to discuss the initial details of the case and agree on how long the hearing will take. An

133

employment tribunal court is different from a criminal court, so there will not be a jury present. It will be you and your legal team, the employee and their legal team, and the judge (possibly a panel of judges) considering the case.

7. At the preliminary hearing, the judge will issue orders on how each side must proceed ahead of the final hearing. You will be given dates by which you as the respondent need to create the "bundle" - which is the collection of documents and evidence that will be called upon during the case. The employee will be given a deadline by which they need to send to you any evidence they wish to use, and this bundle will be finalised by both of you. All evidence must be included that you will use - you cannot present 'surprise' evidence on the day. You will also be given dates by which point your witnesses have to share their witness statements. Witnesses will be asked to write their recollections of the matters involved in the case, and this will be shared with both sides. Witnesses will not be allowed to deviate from these statements during the hearing.

8. On the day of the hearing, you as the respondent will be required to bring clean, unmarked copies of the bundle and witness statements for everyone present (at a minimum your legal team, the claimant and their legal team, the judge(s), and each of the witnesses). The judge will confirm the details of the case with each side, followed by the legal team of each side presenting their case. The judge(s) will then withdraw to review the bundle and consider the details of the case. Once they return, witnesses will then be called in turn to read out their statements, and then have clarifying questions asked first by the legal team that called them as a witness and then by the opposing legal team. The judge(s) may also ask clarifying questions. The legal teams will then take turns in summarising their case. The judge(s) will then deliberate and issue their decision. This can happen on the day or afterwards in writing.

The whole tribunal process can be quite lengthy, with delays at each step. The employment tribunal courts are overloaded with claims, and so it can take a long time for a preliminary hearing to be scheduled, followed by a long wait before the final hearing takes place. As a result, it is worthwhile collecting your documents and considering your witnesses as soon as you become aware a tribunal claim has been filed. While facts are fresh in people's minds, get the details recorded. It may be years before the case is heard in full and memories will fade in the meantime. It is worth bearing in mind that no matter how strong your case is, no tribunal outcome is guaranteed. Get the legal support you need from the start to make sure you can present your case as well as possible. Make sure you have insurance in place if it does not go your way.

Remember that at any point prior to step 8, you could choose to settle outside of court. This would involve you instructing your legal team to contact the claimant and make an offer to settle. These contacts are made "without prejudice", which means any genuine attempts to settle cannot be used as evidence of admission in court. In layman's terms, you cannot be judged as admitting to doing anything wrong by trying to settle outside of court. It can be a difficult decision to settle outside of court, and a variety of factors should be taken into consideration:

1. Your financial position - can you afford to go to court? If you do not have the right insurance in place, your own legal fees can become very expensive, not to mention that of the claimant if you lose. How much would it cost to settle? Is this affordable for you?
2. The strength of your case - your legal team will advise you on this. You may not have done something wrong, but there may be insufficient evidence to demonstrate this. You need to consider the likelihood you will win, and this should factor into your decision on your financial position.
3. The terms of settlement - you can often add certain terms to resolve ongoing issues alongside the settlement, such as a non-disclosure agreement so the claimant can never publicly discuss the dispute or the settlement amount. Remember, all tribunal outcomes are matters of public record. If a claim could be particularly damaging to your reputation, even if you did nothing wrong, then settling may be a way to avoid the spotlight. Conversely, you may wish to publicly demonstrate that you did not do what is being claimed and see it as a way to clear your organisation's name.

4. Impact on your team - beyond the public perception, you need to consider the impact on your team and your organisation's ability to continue beyond the claim. It may be that your team is very close with the claimant and a lengthy tribunal case may cause deep divisions and further unhappiness within your organisation. It may be that your team rallies against the injustice of the claim and it builds morale to see the organisation fight the attack. It may set a precedence that you settle claims, which could lead to more claims being made. You will know your team and you will need to assess their likely response.

There is no hard and fast rule in deciding whether or not to settle. You will need to consider all the factors carefully and then make the right decision for your organisation.

Health and safety

As an employer, you have a duty of care to protect your team members' physical and mental health and wellbeing. This is the right thing to do. From a purely selfish point of view, you are a member of your team and so by protecting your team's physical and mental health, you are protecting yourself. From an economic point of view, investing in your team's physical and mental health and wellbeing will pay dividends over the long term as your team is able to be more productive, build better relationships with your community, and remain loyal to the organisation for longer. From a legal point of view, you must do this. From a humanist point of view, you must do this.

In the UK, the Health and Safety Executive (HSE) has a comprehensive free website that outlines all the different areas you must consider. Health and Safety overall is common sense. As a CEO, you will have ultimate responsibility for the health and safety of your team. Your team members are also individually responsible for following the rules and looking after their own health and safety, and that of their colleagues. You need to assess the risks in your workplace that could impact your team, but also anyone else who visits your workplace. This will be unique to your setting, but a few common risks and hazards are:

- Slips, trips, and falls - these could be caused by steps, uneven surfaces, slips, slippery flooring, poor lighting, obstacles in passageways, etc
- Fire - fires could be sparked by old and faulty equipment, loose paper near ignition sources, stoves and open heaters, overburdened power sockets, etc
- Musculoskeletal injury - this could be caused by poor manual handling of items, unsuitable sitting and desk arrangements, non-ergonomic keyboard and mouses, etc
- Cuts and burns - these could be caused by incorrect use of equipment, kitchen utensils, cleaning chemicals, lone working, etc
- Stress - this is covered in a previous section, but could be caused by poor workload management, insufficient management support, lack of control over work, etc

To create a Health and Safety risk assessment, think through all of the activities that your team members engage in and how physical and/or mental injury could befall them in undertaking those activities. Do not just hypothetically imagine here - engage with your team members. Ask them for their thoughts on when they feel at risk during work and why. Then consider how you can reduce the risk and commit to undertaking the mitigating actions, as far as reasonably possible. You can never eliminate all sources of risk, but you can build in mechanisms to significantly reduce them. Establishing a culture of continuous learning can be very beneficial here, as where unforeseen risks arise you can quickly react with your team to identify and mitigate them as effectively as possible. Once you have identified your risks and mitigating actions, make the commitment to set deadlines for fulfilment and assign responsibility to a team member (often yourself).

Remember also that as an employer, you have a legal requirement to take out Employers' Liability insurance. This exists to offer some support where risks cannot be fully avoided. If you engage with the public in any way and/or sell products, you'll likely need to take out Public and Product Liability insurance as well to compensate them for any unintended public harm you may cause.

Furthermore, think more broadly than just the legal requirements. As previously mentioned, the organisation benefits from a team with good physical and mental health and wellbeing. If there are simple and affordable ways to improve conditions for your team, then do it. These changes do not need to break the bank. For example, in setting up an office, ask your team for their preferences on equipment. You can set a maximum budget for each team member that you can afford, you can even set out just two or three options that meet the legal safety requirements. But then let them have a choice in the matter to fit their personal needs. It sounds simple, but giving your team some freedom of choice will boost morale, which in turn has a positive effect on both physical and mental health and wellbeing.

Finally, a point about 'reasonable'. This word comes up a lot in health and safety guidance as a legal cover-all to avoid placing an undue financial burden on organisations, especially small ones. Reasonable tends to mean affordable, proportionate, and feasible. It does not mean you can avoid a health and safety risk, no questions asked. It provides some flexibility in addressing risks. For example, ideally there would be step-free access all throughout a premises to avoid any slips, trips, and falls. However, if you are renting office space then you cannot remove the step. Even if you owned the building, it might be prohibitively expensive to remove the step (depending on where it is, it could cost tens of thousands). But, you can put down fluorescent tape to demarcate the edge of a step. You can install daylight bulbs so that people can clearly see the steps. You can grit the step (if it is outdoors) in winter to reduce slippery conditions. You can get a portable ramp - or even install a permanent ramp - next to the step to help those with mobility difficulties. In sum, you will always have a spectrum of choices from free and easy to difficult and expensive. 'Reasonable' means you pick the most effective of those choices that are within your available budget and control. It is worth bearing in mind that the expectation is always that you do the best that you can. If you slack off and someone gets hurt, legally you will be in dangerous waters as it will be seen as negligence. Your insurance may not cover it and it could bankrupt the organisation, especially small ones. Also, you will be responsible for someone getting hurt. Financial and legal requirements aside, be a person that cares.

Data protection

In the UK, the Data Protection Act 2018 (DPA) and the UK General Data Protection Regulation 2021 (UK GDPR) set out the data protection framework and principles for processing personal data in the UK. The Information Commissioner's Office (ICO) has an excellent free website that outlines all the latest data protection requirements and legislation, including a hub for small organisations. If you collect, use, hold, or do anything else with personal information, then you need to comply with the data protection law. According to the ICO personal information is "any information that can identify a living person. This could be anything from a name or email address to medical information or a computer's IP address." This pretty much covers all organisations as you will at a minimum have a list of your team's names and email addresses.

Every organisation or sole trader that processes personal information in the UK needs to register with the ICO and pay an annual data protection fee. The fee is tiered based on the size and turnover of the organisation - although charities and small occupational pension schemes always pay the lowest tier regardless.

The seven key principles of data protection legislation are:
- Lawfulness, fairness and transparency - this means you have legal grounds for using the data; you use the data in ways that a person would expect and does not detriment the person; and you make it clear how you will use the data.
- Purpose limitation - this means you make it clear what you intend to use the data for and limit the data usage to only that. It means you need to make the person aware and get their consent before you use their data for any other reasons than originally specified.
- Data minimisation - this means that you only collect data that is relevant and necessary for your stated purpose. You do not collect more data than you need 'just in case'.
- Accuracy - this means that you have processes in place to check the accuracy of personal data you collect and that individuals have the right to rectify any errors in their personal data.

- Storage limitation - this means you have clearly defined timelines for storing the personal data that are justified and you do not hold the data for longer than you need. When you no longer need the personal data, you must securely delete it or anonymise it.
- Integrity and confidentiality - this means you must keep the data secure and protect non-authorised users from accessing the personal data.
- Accountability - this means you need to take responsibility for your use of personal data and demonstrate your compliance with the data protection legislation.

The ICO website delves into the requirements for each of these seven principles and the rights of individuals whose personal data is being used. There are useful guides, toolkits, templates, and quizzes available to ensure you are compliant.

Cyber security

As outlined above, one of the principles of data protection is keeping the data secure. While you may have physical copies of data, such as printed documents stored in filing cabinets, it is likely that most of your data will be kept digitally as well. You will need to create a cyber security policy around keeping your digital data safe. The National Cyber Security Centre has a useful website that contains advice and guidance for different stakeholders, including guidance for those that are self-employed or sole traders; and small and medium organisations.

The main guidance for everyone is to:
1. Create a strong and unique password for your email - your email is usually the gateway to all of your accounts. Therefore, it is vital you keep this password unique so that if another one of your accounts is compromised, the hacker would not be able to use the information there to hack into your email.
2. Create unique passwords for other services, made up of three random words (such as PurpleElephantFlower) - using random words makes passwords more memorable for you, but difficult to guess for someone else.

3. Save your passwords in a password manager to keep them safe and accessible - if you have a unique password for every account then you will soon start to forget them. Secure password managers exist, such as in your browser, where you can safely store them for future reference.
4. Turn on two-factor authentication - this will usually mean that when you log into a system (such as your email or your database), you will need to confirm your identity using a different system (such as a code texted to your phone). The benefit of this is that if someone cracked your password, they would not be able to access your account unless they also had access to your phone for example.
5. Update your devices - all devices and systems will release software updates that include updated security measures. Out of date software, apps, and operating systems are weak and vulnerable to hacks.
6. Backup your data - if you have vital information, make sure there are separate copies of it stored in different places. For example, you can have backup printed copies locked in your office or digital copies saved on an external hard drive. Having backups can limit the impact of having a system hacked because you do not lose access to everything.

Given the proliferation of cyber attacks, it is important that you not only protect yourself but that you have an effective response in place in case of a cyber security attack. This should be part of your business continuity plan (see section Managing Risk) and should include the following stages:
1. Identify - how will you identify if a cyber attack is underway or has occurred? Who monitors this?
2. Assess - what the symptoms are? What may have been the cause? What systems are impacted? How widespread is it? Which stakeholders are affected?
3. Respond - who will be notified? How will you remove the vulnerabilities leading to the incident?
4. Report - you will need to capture all of the information gathered in steps 1-3 and report it to the relevant governing body within your organisation. If personal data has been compromised, you may need to report it to the individuals

whose data has been compromised, the ICO, and possibly even the police.

5. Review - after the conclusion of the incident, you will need to discuss it in detail, review the response, and then construct a Process Improvement Plan to prevent a recurrence of similar incidents.

Cyber attacks do not target only large organisations. Small organisations and charities have increasingly been targeted as the cyber attackers assume they will be less protected. Keeping your data secure is not just a legal requirement, it is an essential undertaking for an organisation's survival.

Income generation

As the CEO, your role in income generation will likely be reserved to strategic partnerships and key clients/customers/funders (for simplicity, these will all be referred to as clients). If you have more than a handful of clients, then you should designate or hire a team member to lead on income generation as it is a very time-intensive and critical function of any organisation. No matter how important your work is, if you do not have sufficient income, you cease to exist. As your role will be limited, this section only focuses on strategic income generation.

Strategic income generation

As CEO, you will likely only be involved in securing major clients/customers/funders for your organisation. This is partly because as CEO, you will be so busy looking after all the other sections outlined in this field guide that it would be damaging to the organisation for you to spend time on minor income generation. You have limited time and so you need to balance that time across all the mission-critical areas of running your organisation. Saving you as a reserve for major clients will also have the added benefit of flattering the major clients with your attention, which will make them more inclined to talk with you. There is power and prestige inherent in the CEO title, so even if you do not feel particularly important in a tiny team in a tiny organisation, others will elevate you in their eyes purely because of the title. As previously mentioned, do not let this go to your head, it is just a title after all. You are not inherently better than anyone else just because of the title. But do utilise the effect as a tool for the benefit of your organisation. In approaching these major clients, follow the below key steps.

Identify your target clients

You need to identify which potential major clients you will approach to focus your efforts on those that have the highest impact on your organisation and are most likely to have successful outcomes. To do this, you need to reduce all potential major clients through the following filters (Miller et al., 2011):

1. Fit with your values and attitude to your product and/or service - if this fundamental fit does not exist, then they are

unlikely to identify with your brand and they will not be engaged by your communications (see Communications section for more details).

2. Create a profile based on your best and worst existing clients (if you have any) to determine what characteristics they share, so you can actively pursue clients that fit the best profile and avoid those that fit the worst profile.

3. Test your potential major clients against these best and worst profiles, to determine who you should cultivate and who you should consider distancing yourself to avoid wasting time. Give each potential major client a ranking from +5 (best) to -5 (worst).

Based on this filtering, you should be left with a list of potential major clients, ranked in order of most valuable to your organisation. This forms the basis of your sales funnel, prioritising who you should approach in the first instance.

Set income generation objectives

As with any strategy, you need to have clear aims for what you are trying to achieve. With your prioritised list of clients, you will then need to identify your specific objectives for each client. These objectives should be SMART - Specific, Measurable, Achievable, Realistic, and Timely. You should consider the timeline across which you want to generate income as part of this objective setting. Are you wanting a one-off sale/grant? Or are you trying to build a longer-term commitment? You do not want to shoot yourself in the foot by pressing so hard for a sale right now, that a potential long-term customer is turned off and will never work with you again.

Analyse your current position

Next, you need to honestly analyse where you stand with each potential client.

First, identify all of the people who have to give their approval or input before your objective can be achieved. Miller and Heiman (2011) identify four key roles you will need to consider:

1. Economic buying influence - the person who gives final approval for the spending of money, for example, a board of

trustees; CEO; the head of a department. They hold the pursestrings and ultimately will have to be convinced to open them.
2. Use buying influence - the person(s) who will actually use your product and/or service once it has been purchased. If you are 'selling' a charitable activity to secure a grant, the use buying influence here would be the person(s) who feels the benefit of having supported a worthy cause.
3. Technical buying influence - the person(s) who screen out suppliers based on technical details. Their role is to find reasons to say no, and you will need to find ways to address their requirements so they cannot say no.
4. Coach / Lobbyist - the person(s) who wants to work with you and convince the others to say yes. This person may not exist when you are considering a potential client and part of your approach may be to cultivate and create a coach.

Once these roles are identified, you will need to think through what the needs, pains, and gains are of each of these individuals. What are the aims they are trying to achieve? What do they need to achieve the aims? What stands in their way or hinders their achievement (pains)? What could improve their ability to achieve (gains)?

A further key question to consider is what do the individuals in those roles think about their position? Miller and Heiman (2011) explain that each role may perceive their position in four main ways:
1. Growth - the person(s) are looking to improve their position.
2. Trouble - the person(s) is looking to avoid a problem quickly and effectively.
3. Even keel - the person(s) is satisfied with their current position and not looking to change - this would be a red flag for your sale as you will need to convince them that there is a problem or a need for change before you can convince them that your product and/or service can address it.
4. Overconfident - the person(s) believes that their reality is better than it is and so they do not perceive a need for change. Again, this is a possible red flag as you will need to persuade this person that they do not have a correct grasp on reality, which does not always go well.

Analyse your value proposition

Next you need to consider how your current product and/or service fits into the four roles' needs, pains, and gains. This will form the basis of how you approach each role to convince them that your product and/or service is the right choice for them. It is important that your product and/or service is actually right for your client. You want to create a win-win, where you generate the income you need and they get something that benefits them. Do not dupe people into something that they do not need.

If you identify gaps in your product and/or service and the roles' needs, pains, gains, it is a good opportunity to reflect on whether they are the right client for you. If you truly believe they are, then it is a good prompt for you to consider whether you need to change your product/service to better meet your intended clients' needs. There is no point forging ahead if you know there are unresolved issues. If you can identify them, then the client will 100 per cent question it as well. They will then likely say no, and your efforts and opportunity will be wasted.

Create and implement your action plan

With your analysis complete, you then need to plan out how you will approach the client. In some cases, this step will be incredibly straightforward. For example, a grant funder will have an application process that they rigidly enforce, so you just need to follow it and clearly communicate your value proposition tailored to the key roles through each stage of their process. In these cases, always pay attention to their rules and requirements, and respect them. People will be looking for a reason to say no, do not annoy them before they even consider you.

Where such a structure does not exist, then you need to be more creative. You need to map out how you will reach the economic buying influence to get them to sign off on your product and/or service. You can approach them directly, sending an email or giving a phone call to the economic buying influence or use buying influence. You can clearly outline the benefits and see what they say. This can work, but most likely your email will get marked as spam and the receptionist will screen your call.

You can approach them indirectly, setting up a relationship with someone at the organisation, who can then introduce you and recommend you to the economic buying influence. This is someone you cultivate into a coach, but could also be a use buying influence or a technical buying influence. Networking plays a key role here and can add credibility to you as part of that initial contact. You should be upfront about your intentions as no one likes to be unwittingly used. This approach takes longer but can be more fruitful and lead to longer-term income generation streams. It can also build your reputation, which can organically lead to income generation as clients talk to one another and recommend you.

Building partnerships

When you are looking to build a partnership with another organisation, remember that at the end of the day you are dealing with people. You are trying to convince several people at the other organisation that you personally, and by extension your organisation, are someone they want to work with. So: be nice.

Be polite, be respectful, be responsive, be truthful, and follow through on your commitments. Partnerships are built on people wanting to work with people they like.

Consider both parties' needs, not just how you can get what you want from the arrangement. Take the time to get to know them, and understand what they need to achieve, what motivates them, what they wish to gain from the partnership, and what issues they wish to address. Work through how the partnership can help them achieve their goals. It is possible there are more ways you can support one another than you initially anticipated, and taking the time to understand them will help tease out these nuances.

Do not disappear the moment your needs are met. If you have made commitments, stick to them. While the partnership may be time-limited, the relationship with the people at the other organisation will continue. You may encounter them in the future in a different role, with a different power dynamic. Your past behaviour will influence their future responses to you. Do not shoot your future self in the foot now.

Treat your partners like people, not faceless companies. Get to know the people at the company. Build a relationship. For example, when you meet them outside of meetings and engage in friendly small talk, you may learn they have a child or engage in a certain hobby. If you make a note of this at the time and then ask about it the next time you see them, they will feel valued and seen. Giving another person your full attention and listening to them can be a rare experience and is always appreciated. Find ways you can be useful beyond the immediate organisational partnership. You may be able to introduce them to someone in your network that can help with a tangential professional or personal need. Again, this should not be done solely so you can then elicit a favour from them. It is part of relationship building and should be done without an expectation of return.

Thank your partners. Give them honest and sincere appreciation. Show them the impact of your partnership. Do not wait until the end of the partnership to do this. Give small updates throughout to demonstrate the progress being made. As Dale Carnegie (2006) wrote, the deepest urge in human nature is 'the desire to be important.' Demonstrating the importance of your partnership will motivate all involved to keep pushing forward.

Ultimately, this will help create ambassadors for your organisation within the partner company. They will work harder to make your partnership successful. They will also look for mutually beneficial ways you can work together in the future. It will also make day-to-day work that much more enjoyable as you will have built meaningful relationships with others outside of your organisation. It is always nice to have a friend.

Managing risk

In organisations, as in life, every decision has inherent risks. It is important to find a way to manage those risks so you do not become stuck in a quagmire of indecision. Risk management should be part of all of your decision making. All of the previous sections have within them risk management strategies, for example:

- Market analysis as part of strategic planning: helps you stay abreast of developments in your sector that may influence your organisation. The more information you are able to review, the more you reduce the likelihood of 'unknown unknowns' that could destabilise plans.
- Financial planning: reduces the risk of running out of funds.
- Health and safety: identifying ways to avoid injuring your team's health and wellbeing.
- Self-care and good management: reduce the likelihood of you or your team making careless mistakes.

This approach to risk should be captured in three key documents:

1. Strategic plan: As part of your strategic planning, you should identify the key risks that are inherent in your strategy. For each risk, you should create a targeted strategy of how you will monitor the risk, mitigate the risk, and limit the impact of the risk. Example risks to consider: loss of expected income; inability to maintain a suitable staff profile; loss of data; non-compliance with regulation; damage to reputation; malicious threat.

2. Risk monitor: Building on the risks identified in your strategic plan, you should create a spreadsheet that categorises the risks; the potential causes of the risk; anticipated timing; probability of occurrence (rate from 1 unlikely to 5 certain); anticipated impact (rate from 1 low to 3 high); list the mitigating actions that have been or will be taken to address the risk; further actions that need to be taken; and identify the responsible team member that will monitor the risk. This document should not be static, it should be updated as you become aware of risks and implement new mitigating actions. It should be reviewed by your governing body at least once a quarter.

3. Business continuity plan: For each risk that is identified as having a moderate to high impact on the organisation, you should develop a further business continuity plan that details the actions you will take if and when the risk should occur. This allows your team to act swiftly and decisively during a time of crisis. Each risk should be presented as a scenario, with step by step instructions of who will do what and when with all relevant information to undertake the instructions. For example, an incident on the premises (e.g. fire, flood, or any other disaster that renders the office inaccessible) you would need different scenarios depending on whether the incident occurred during office hours or outside of office hours. The immediate response would likely include evacuation, confirmation of the incident, calling emergency services, recording any injury in accordance with Health and Safety regulations, alerting staff not present, and assessing the damage. Once those immediate steps are taken, longer-term business continuity steps would need to start, for example: establishing alternative working locations, diverting telephones and post, informing your insurance provider, and informing your community. Finally, you would need a plan for recovery. While these plans will be fairly generic, they provide a firm basis on which customised plans can be built in response to an actual incident.

In all of your risk assessments, you must remember that you will never eliminate all risks. You must also be aware of your own biases when deciding on the probability and impact of risks. As mentioned in the strategy section, the availability heuristic will be at play, which influences your ability to judge the likelihood of a risk occurring based on your ability to imagine it happening. If you find it difficult to imagine something, such as a global pandemic causing national lockdowns for 18+ months, then you will think it unlikely to occur and not plan for it. That is why most organisations had to scramble to create a pandemic continuity plan in early 2020 as COVID-19 spread across the world. Even as the pandemic killed thousands, many organisations did not create a response plan until the virus showed up in their own country as they could not conceive of the threat. After all, a global pandemic of that scale had not occurred since the Spanish Flu in 1918.

As Nassim Nicholas Taleb (2007) warns with his work on highly improbable events and the fallacy of randomness: there is a difference between "has never gone down" and "never goes down". What is highly improbable may still occur. The present is not a reliable predictor of what will happen in the future. In Taleb's words, if there were surprises and unexpected occurrences in the past which were markedly different to the time before it (what Taleb refers to as "the past's past"), then "why should our future resemble our current past?" Regardless of your preparation, black swans will occur, unknown unknowns will have an impact, and your organisation will be exposed to risks and threats. However, your risk management strategies will help reduce the impact and may mean the difference between closure and continuity.

For all you cannot mitigate, insurance will help fill in the gaps. At a minimum, you should consider contents insurance (if your organisation has a physical premise(s)); equipment breakdown (if you own any equipment, including computers or specialist machines); business interruption (to cover any business continuity issues); and money and assault (if you operate with larger sums of cash). Most insurance companies will bundle the above together with the necessary health and safety insurance categories for businesses, so you do not need to deal with multiple companies to cover all of your insurance needs. Unless you need any further specialist insurance, it is worth shopping around to find the best deal. If your organisation is fairly stable year in, year out then your costs should stay fairly stable as well. That said, consider shopping around for a better deal every 3 to 5 years. It can be a surprisingly effective way to keep costs low.

Communications

Communications are an integral part of any organisation. It often gets overlooked in small organisations, being written off as a 'nice to have'. That is simply not true. No organisation exists in a bubble and you have to communicate with others to carry out your work and generate income. When you start to communicate with the outside world, you need someone to answer the call. This may be you if you have a very small organisation. However, this is a useful role to delegate to a set team member(s) as they will serve as the gateway to the organisation and you will need someone who is always available during opening hours.

Define the audience(s)

Communication is not about shouting endlessly into the void, in the hopes that someone will answer back. Especially with a small organisation, you need to be extremely focused and targeted with your communications. You may be tempted to explore all options to identify what works, but with limited resources, you'll likely end up doing a mediocre (at best) job and burning out your comms team member.

You need to identify the specific audience types you want to communicate with. The audiences you need to work with will be defined through your organisational strategy. This could be individuals, groups, organisations, governments, etc. Work through their typical characteristics to build you an audience profile or persona. You will need to undertake research here so you can tie your audience persona to real information and data. What is their median age? Gender identity? Level of education? Income? Location? Accessibility needs? Interests (beyond your organisation)? Why do they care about your organisation and your product/service?

Think through what you want from each audience type. For example, you may want customers to buy your product or use your service. You may want foundation managers to grant your charity funds. You may want local business owners to partner with your organisation.

As with your overall strategy, you should define key aims for each audience you wish to communicate with.

Identify the appropriate communications channel

Once you have defined your intended audience(s), you will need to identify the most appropriate communications channels you need to use to reach them. Again, you will need to do your research to understand what channels are being used by people that fit within your audience personas.

There is such a proliferation of communication channels, that each main channel has a number of sub-options, which allows you to specialise and better focus your energies on your desired audience(s). For example:

- Telephone: Landline? Mobile? Video call app? Your intended audience might not trust an organisation with a mobile number instead of a landline. Or they may feel more comfortable sending texts rather than speaking on the phone. This will be influenced by your resources and premises as well - you may be on the move a lot and prefer a portable option. Or you may be office based with a telephone line as part of your rental agreement.
- Websites: what devices are your audiences predominantly using to look at websites? Desktops? Laptops? Tablets? Mobile devices? This will influence the layout and design of your website to make it easier to use with a mouse and keyboard vs fingers; external screens vs small portable screens; reading on the go means shorter content vs reading at home means they have more time to explore.
- Social media: Are you going to use Facebook, Twitter, LinkedIn, Instagram, Youtube, Snapchat, or Tik Tok? Are you going to create your own app to directly communicate with users? Each social media platform has a widely different profile of users, with new popular platforms emerging and being bought every few years. Are you going to create content and/ or use the platform for advertising?
- Print media: are you writing press releases for local, national, and/or international news? Are you targeting local

newsletters or flyer drops? Are you putting up posters around a city?

Free reports on different communication channels are constantly being written by communications and marketing experts based on usage analytics. The most up to date ones can be easily found through an online search to help you zero in on the right option for your resources and your audiences.

Creating brand identity

Once you know who you want to speak to and where you will reach them, you need to think about how you will speak to them. This is a step prior to you figuring out exactly what you will say. You need to consider the persona of your organisation. To do this, you need to think through the following four areas:

1. Essence - what one to three words capture your organisation's essence? Some famous examples are: Coca-Cola - Refreshment; Apple - Simplicity; Disney - Magical. What is the unique feeling you want your audiences to have when they interact with you? What will be at the heart of every message, to ensure consistency in your communications? Remember, people interpret consistency as trustworthy and authentic. Inconsistency is felt to be suspicious and untrustworthy. Your purpose, mission, aims, and values will help in refining the words down into something that captures the organisation's essence.
2. Personality, image, and tone of voice - once you have your essence, you need to define your organisation's character. How will you present yourself externally? Will you be formal or informal? Friendly or distant? Funny or serious? Opinionated or factual? Again, this will need to be consistent from the way your team interacts in person at meetings to the messages posted online. Consistency is key.
3. Visual expression - the organisation's character can then guide the visual identity of the organisation from the logo to the colour scheme to the font to the imagery used. A consistent visual identity will reinforce your messages and make your audiences feel like they know you. An inconsistent visual expression can make people confused and suspect a

scam. For example, a serious organisational character would not suit bright, neon colours. A joyful, friendly organisational character would not suit Times New Roman font.

Graphic designers and marketing consultants can be a big help in defining the organisation's brand identity. If you are a social organisation or charity, big marketing firms often have pro bono programmes where they help small organisations for free. Other small organisations may benefit from using freelancers, who can be contacted through online platforms such as Fiverr and Upwork.

Telling the organisation's story

Once you have the who, why, where, and how of your communications strategy, you then need to tackle the what. What are you going to say?

This will be unique to your organisation, your communication aims, your audiences, your channels, and your brand identity. But there are six principles (Heath and Heath, 2008) that you should consider in making sure what you say gets remembered:
1. Simplicity - do not overcomplicate your messages. List out all the different facets of the information you are trying to communicate, and then try to strip back sentences and words until you are left with the essence of the message and nothing else. As the famous quote by Antoine de Saint-Exupery goes: "Perfection is achieved, not when there is nothing more to add, but when there is nothing left to take away."
2. Unexpectedness - you want to generate interest and curiosity by surprising your audience. In *Made to Stick*, Heath recommends that you identify the unexpected implications of your core message and then find a way to communicate your message in a way that is counterintuitive. This will cause your audience to pause and consider the message for a moment longer, which will increase the likelihood of engagement.
3. Concreteness - avoid talking in abstract terms. Link to real, concrete images and concepts that can be visualised and absorbed easily.
4. Credibility - your message needs to be credible without relying on your brand authority. This is where consistency

comes in and linkage to other credible sources. Statistics and/ or testimonials for others here can reinforce your message.

5. Emotions - create an emotional connection with your audience. Heath's excellent example is that "people don't buy quarter-inch drill bits. They buy quarter-inch holes so they can hang their children's pictures." Be aware of how you combine the emotional connection with the credibility information provided. Statistics can cause people to approach a topic from an analytical mindset, which can hinder emotional connection. It is best to establish the emotional connection first and then use your statistics to establish credibility afterwards to reinforce the message.

6. Stories - stories are a powerful way to share information. We may struggle to remember a series of facts, but we are more likely to remember them if they are connected through a story. There are many ways you can integrate stories into your messaging, for example, the story of the organisation's set up, the story of a customer/beneficiary accessing your product/services, and the story of the benefit you have created. When considering what story to tell, identify all of the potential protagonists - these can be people, objects, or concepts. You could tell your story from the perspective of the problem you are trying to solve and how it resents all of your efforts.

Thinking through the above principles will help narrow down the central messages of your organisation. Once you have the content, you will need to think through how these will be adapted for each audience and each communication channel. As mentioned throughout, consistency is key even as you adapt your messaging. You should consider how each communication channel will interact with each other so that your message is reinforced if an audience engages with you in more than one way. For example, if you share an announcement on your social media, does your website reinforce the message with more details? Are the team members who answer the telephone aware of the announcement so they can answer questions if someone calls up?

Finally, as with any organisational decision, you should undertake a risk analysis of your communications strategy. How might someone misinterpret your message? Are there cultural/political/social movements taking place that your message may inadvertently link to? Is your acronym slang for a concept that you do not want to be associated with? What would be the implications of this? When you become aware of risks, find ways to mitigate them. For example, testing out your messaging with trusted representatives of your audiences to see how they respond. Be open to changing your mind and adapting your messaging, no matter how much time and effort you put into it. Backlash and outrage will take much more time and effort to resolve.

Monitor, analyse, and refine

Finally, do not forget to monitor the impact of your messaging once you start communicating. If you are using digital communication channels, then you can freely access the statistics of your channel. You will be able to see the number of views and interactions, the characteristics of your audience, and possibly even information about their location and the devices they used to access your content. You will be able to see how these statistics change depending on the different communications activities you undertake. Non-digital communication channels can be tracked more manually - for example, you can track how many telephone calls you received after you posted flyers. You can create categories for different types of telephone calls and then tally how many of each type you get over a set time period.

From this data, you can see trends emerging around what type of messages generates interaction (positive vs. negative), who responds to your messages, and what external circumstances can drive engagement or dry it up. You can then use this to refine your communications strategy and refine each step outlined in this section.

PART 4

MOVING ON

Just as important as knowing what to do while you are CEO, is to recognise when it is no longer appropriate for you to be the CEO. Like a good houseguest, you need to know when it is time for you to leave. How you handle this will greatly impact the organisation's ability to survive and thrive in the long term.

Succession planning

Even before you begin to think about moving on, you should plan for your succession. After all, your leaving may not be within your control. Unfortunately, accidents do happen and you do not want to be a single point of failure for your organisation. Your team and your board need to know what to do if anything were to happen to you.

A first step is to create a team skills register, which identifies the key skills required to keep the organisation running. These will be specific to your organisation's activities, but the following will likely be relevant for all organisations:

- Company and legal issues
- Finances
- HR and policies
- Income generation
- Communications
- Managing IT
- Health and Safety

To reduce the risk to the organisation if something happened to any team member, yourself included, you will need to ensure that at least two or more team members have the ability to cover each essential function. This can inform the training and development you invest in for your team and new hires.

While someone might have the skills to cover, they may not have the knowledge. Therefore, it is useful to keep notes on the different essential tasks that you fulfil as CEO. For example, financial management. What steps do you follow to forecast the organisation's annual budget? Who is responsible for payroll and what are their contact details? Which day(s) of the month do salaries get paid? These notes should be shared with your second in command and/or the Chair of your governing body. Alongside this, you should collate all of your passwords in a password manager (see Cyber Security section), which again the Chair of your governing body should know how to access. Collectively, this will protect the organisation and keep the cogs turning in case something happens to you. At a basic level, this will set the foundations for your succession as it will allow others to step in while your replacement is found.

You can build on this foundation by planning more precisely who you think should succeed you. As with any other role, you should create a job description for the post of CEO and the required person specification. You can then consider whether there is someone already within your team that can be supported to take on the role of CEO in the future. The likely candidates (depending on your organisational structure) will be someone you informally turn to as your second-in-command; someone who is formally recognised as your deputy in their job description; or one of the senior managers that you work closely with to run the organisation.

When identified, you can use a formal performance evaluation meeting (such as an appraisal or supervision) or an informal management touchpoint (such as a weekly one-to-one) to check in with the team member to explore their career aspirations and whether they had considered becoming a CEO in future. If they are interested, you can then offer to mentor them so that they have the right skills and knowledge to step into your shoes should you ever leave. You should create a formalised structure for this mentoring, to manage expectations on both sides about content and time commitment. You could invite them to shadow you in key meetings; you can set aside an hour each month to discuss in detail a different facet of running an organisation; you can send them on training programmes to address any areas for improvement. (See section on Development for further detail).

Be aware, that by raising the possibility with them, you may expand their career aspirations and set an internal timeline by which point they want to become a CEO. If you do not leave prior to this time, they may choose to leave the organisation to pursue the opportunity elsewhere.

Know when to leave

The following may be signs that it is time for you to consider moving on:

- You feel pulled towards a new challenge, new opportunity, and/or new organisation
- You are no longer interested in your role and/or the organisation - you may even resent it
- You find yourself altering the organisation's strategy away from what would be best to what you feel you can personally deliver
- You do not feel like you can keep up with the demands of the role
- The organisation is changing direction and you do not feel you have the skills or knowledge to lead it into its new phase

These signs do not necessarily have to result in you leaving. It could be that with more training and mentoring you could lead the organisation in a new direction. With better support from your board and/or improved delegation to your team, you could rise up to the challenges and cope with your role. You may need to reconnect with your passion for the organisation's aims to reignite your interest in your role. Ultimately, you will know whether you want to put in the effort to make your current situation better, or whether you think it is time for a new opportunity.

Effective handover

When you do decide you want to leave, you should start planning your handover to your successor. The first step of which is to accept that by leaving, you are giving up long-term control over the organisation. This is a significant mental and emotional step. As a small organisation CEO, you will likely have put your (hopefully metaphoric) blood, sweat, and tears into the organisation. You will likely feel very attached to the organisation and not want to see someone else undo all of your hard work. However, if you decide to leave, you have to let this need for control go. You will have to start to defer to the continuing team members and governing body on decisions. You will not need to live with those decisions - they will.

The second step is a similar mental and emotional step. You have to let your ego go. You may think you were the best thing that ever happened to the organisation and that only someone identical to you could ever hope to replace you. You are wrong. You may have been the best thing that ever happened to the organisation when you joined. But just like you, the organisation will have changed over the intervening years. It will likely need new knowledge, new experiences, and new skills to take it forward. And again, it is not your decision what that will be. You can always advise, but it will not be your decision. So do not expect your clone to replace you. Do not take it as a personal affront if you are replaced by someone completely different. You have decided to leave for pastures new, let the organisation explore new pastures as well.

With that emotional work out of the way, you should next inform the Chair of the governing body of your decision to leave (or whomever else is assigned as your direct line manager). Be magnanimous, positive, and sensitive in handing in your notice. From a selfish point of view, you will be reliant on the governing body for job references; if you are moving to a new job in the same sector you may need to work with them in the future; and you will still be working with them for a while during your notice period. No point in burning bridges just for the sake of it.

Once you have communicated your decision, ask the Chair how they would like:
- the rest of the governing body, your staff team, and external stakeholders to be informed about your departure
- you to handover to your successor
- you to leave your ongoing projects
- you to be involved in the recruitment of your successor (if at all).

Remember, it is the Chair's decisions that matter now, not so much yours. You can advise, but the final say is now theirs. Stick to your agreement.

Alongside whatever is agreed, it is a good idea to expand on the succession notes outlined in the section above into a full handover document. In this handover document, you should cover the following:

- Overview of your different duties and responsibilities - detailing key contacts; timelines; resources and where to find them; passwords
- Current issues and outstanding actions - preferably prioritised in order of urgency
- Intended future plans - what you would have like to get done had you stayed at the organisation longer
- Key facts about the organisation - in a small organisation, you may hold in your brain part of the institution's memory. If you leave, that may be lost. Try to capture any of the history that you know within the handover document to keep that institutional memory alive.

Once you have the first draft of this handover document, share it with your Chair of the governing body and senior team members to identify any areas that are missing or that need to be expanded upon.

As you work through your notice period, try to tie up any loose ends as far as possible. Try to avoid handing over any pressing issues or disagreements to your succession. Consider how a new person will approach all elements of your role, including the physical and digital resources you keep. Organise your files, both physical and digital. Prune out files that are no longer relevant or required, making sure there is still a trail for your successor to understand your decision making and past events. It can be useful to include a file map within the handover document to direct your successor to where they can find key information.

Alongside this, progressively ramp down your responsibilities as your departure date draws near. Identify key team members who will be responsible for continuing your work during the transition to a new leader. Mentor and guide them on how they can take over your duties, and be on hand to answer any questions as they take on their new tasks.

As you near your departure date, make sure you mark the occasion with a leaving gathering for the team. William Bridges's (1991)

164

research and work with organisations has shown the psychological importance for people to mark the end of something to be able to effectively move on: "you have to end before you can begin". Prepare a few positive comments for the team, and thank people for their work and your time together. Buy a round of drinks or bring in a cake. It will help them move on and it will help you let go.

If there will be an overlapping period between you leaving and your successor starting, you can work with them to plan out an induction programme, the same as you would when recruiting a new team member. Guide them through the different facets of your job, provide contextual background, and answer any questions. Agree upfront how you will handle transferring authority to them so they know when they will have to start to have the final sign off on matters.

If there is no overlap between your notice period and your successor's, then decide how much you want to be available to them. It is nice to offer to take your successor out for lunch after they have had a couple of weeks on the job. In this informal environment, you can answer their questions and concerns. Be mindful of unduly influencing them towards your viewpoints. Present the facts as you see them and let them make up their own minds, especially when it comes to team members. As previously mentioned, people tend to use a change in CEO as an opportunity to reinvent themselves so do not deny them that possibility.

You may find yourself with little to do during your final days on the job. This is a sign of an effective handover. Let go of your ego and reach out to your team, do the odd jobs that need to be done. Find ways to deliver value - after all, you are still being paid. Give yourself the space to relax, recover, let go, and prepare yourself mentally for your next step.

ACKNOWLEDGEMENTS

This book started out like most books written during the pandemic: as a lockdown project to keep me sane. I have been fortunate to have several people support me (at a safe distance) throughout the process. Thank you to Lucy Johnstone for being the first person to hear my idea for the field guide and encouraging me to go for it. Thank you to Mary Galeti and Rick Thompson who reviewed the initial list of contents and gave recommendations on additional elements to include. Thank you to my fellow small organisation CEOs Michelle Marie Bradley, Mark Freeman, Debbie Geraghty, and Nick Milner who reviewed the first draft and gave invaluable feedback to smooth out the rough edges.

Thank you to my brother Donát and father Zsolt for reading my drafts, giving honest feedback, and always supporting me. And a huge thank you to my wonderful partner Chris Rosser, without whom no one else would be reading these words.

REFERENCES

ACAS. "Manage staff redundancies." *ACAS,* https://www.acas.org.uk/manage-staff-redundancies.

ACAS. "Work and employment law advice." *ACAS,* https://www.acas.org.uk/advice.

Agarwal, P. *Sway: Unravelling Unconscious Bias.* Bloomsbury USA, 2020.

Allen, D. *Getting Things Done: The Art of Stress-free Productivity.* Little, Brown Book Group Limited, 2015.

Almquist, E., et al. "The elements of value." *Harvard Business Review,* vol. 94, no. 9, 2016, pp. 46-52.

Brackett, M. *Permission to Feel.* Quercus, 2019.

Bridges, W. *Managing Transitions: Making the Most of Change.* Addison-Wesley, 1991.

Brown, B. *Dare to Lead: Brave Work, Tough Conversations, Whole Hearts.* Ebury Publishing, 2018.

Bungay Stanier, M. *The Coaching Habit: Say Less, Ask More & Change the Way You Lead Forever.* Page Two Books, Incorporated, 2016.

Carnegie, D. *How to Win Friends and Influence People.* Vermilion, 2006.

Doerr, J. E. *Measure what Matters: OKRs - the Simple Idea that Drives 10x Growth.* Portfolio Penguin, 2018.

Downey, M. *Effective Modern Coaching: The Principles and Art of Successful Business Coaching.* LID Publishing, 2014.

Drotter, S., et al. *The Leadership Pipeline: How to Build the Leadership Powered Company*. Wiley, 2011.

Dyer, W. W. *Pulling Your Own Strings*. Arrow, 1990.

Farmer, P. "How to implement the Thriving at Work mental health standards in your workplace." *Mind*, 2017, https://www.mind.org.uk/media-a/5762/mind_taw_a4_report_july18_final_webv2.pdf.

Goffee, R., and G. Jones. "Managing Authenticity: The Paradox of Great Leadership." *Harvard Business Review*, vol. 83, no. 12, 2005, pp. 86-94.

Goldsmith, M. *What Got You Here Won't Get You There: How Successful People Become Even More Successful*. Profile Books, 2008.

Goleman, D. *Emotional Intelligence: Why It Can Matter More Than IQ*. Bantam Books, 1995.

Goleman, D. "Leadership That Gets Results." *Harvard Business Review*, vol. 78, no. 2, 2000, pp. 78-90.

Goleman, D. "What makes a leader?" *Harvard Business Review*, no. Best of HBR on Emotionally Intelligent Leadership, 2008, pp. 3-14.

Goleman, D., and R. Boyatzis. "Social intelligence and the biology of leadership." *Harvard Business Review*, no. Best of HBR on Emotionally Intelligent Leadership, 2008, pp. 42-50.

Hatch, M. J. "The dynamics of organizational culture." *Academy of Management*, vol. 18, no. 4, 1993, pp. 657-693.

Health and Safety Executive. "Health and Safety Made Simple: The basics for your business." *HSE*, https://www.hse.gov.uk/simple-health-safety/index.htm.

Heath, D., and C. Heath. *Made to Stick: Why Some Ideas Take Hold and Others Come Unstuck*. Arrow Books, 2008.

Heffernan, M. *Dare to Disagree*. June 2012. *TED: Ideas Worth Spreading*, https://www.ted.com/talks/margaret_heffernan_dare_to_disagree.

HMRC. "Expenses and benefits: A to Z." *GOV.UK*, https://www.gov.uk/expenses-and-benefits-a-to-z.

HMRC. "Workplace pensions: About workplace pensions." *GOV.UK*, https://www.gov.uk/workplace-pensions.

Howard-Grenville, J., et al. "Liminality as Cultural Process for Cultural Change." *Organization Science*, vol. 22, no. 2, 2011, pp. 522-539.

Information Commissioner's Office. "For organisations." *ICO*, https://ico.org.uk/for-organisations/.

Information Commissioner's Office. "GDPR principles." *ICO*, https://ico.org.uk/for-organisations/guide-to-data-protection/guide-to-the-general-data-protection-regulation-gdpr/principles/.

Information Commissioner's Office. "SME web hub." *ICO*, https://ico.org.uk/for-organisations/sme-web-hub/.

Kahneman, D. *Thinking, Fast and Slow*. Farrar, Straus and Giroux, 2012.

Kets de Vries, M.F.R. "The Leadership Mystique." *Academy of Management Executive*, vol. 8, no. 3, 1994, pp. 73-89.

Kline, N. *Time to Think: Listening to Ignite the Human Mind*. Octopus Books, 1999.

Meyer, E., and R. Hastings. *No Rules Rules: Netflix and the Culture of Reinvention*. Random House UK Limited, 2022.

Miller, R. B., et al. *The New Strategic Selling*. Kogan Page, 2011.

National Cyber Security Centre. "Self employed & sole traders." *NCSC*, https://www.ncsc.gov.uk/section/information-for/self-employed-sole-traders.

National Cyber Security Centre. "Small & medium sized organisations." *NCSC*, https://www.ncsc.gov.uk/section/information-for/small-medium-sized-organisations.

OfNS. "CPIH ANNUAL RATE." *Office for National Statistics*, https://www.ons.gov.uk/economy/inflationandpriceindices/timeseries/l55o/mm23.

O'Neill, M. B. *Executive Coaching with Backbone and Heart: A Systems Approach to Engaging Leaders with Their Challenges.* Wiley, 2007.

Pink, D. H. *When: The Scientific Secrets of Perfect Timing.* Canongate Books, 2019.

Porter, M. "The Five Competitive Forces that Shape Strategy." *Harvard Business Review*, vol. 86, no. 1, 2008, pp. 78-93.

Schmidt, E., et al. *Trillion Dollar Coach: The Leadership Handbook of Silicon Valley's Bill Campbell.* Hodder & Stoughton, 2020.

Sinek, S. *Start with why: How Great Leaders Inspire Everyone to Take Action.* Portfolio / Penguin, 2011.

Taleb, N. N. *Fooled by Randomness: The Hidden Role of Chance in Life and in the Markets.* Penguin Adult, 2007.

Tsui, A. S., et al. "Unpacking the relationship between CEO leadership behaviour and organizational culture." *The Leadership Quarterly*, vol. 17, 2006, pp. 113-137.

Walker, M. *Why We Sleep: The New Science of Sleep and Dreams.* Penguin Books, 2018.

Whitmore, J. *Coaching for Performance: The Principles and Practice of Coaching and Leadership.* 5th ed., Mobius, 2017.

Williams, M., et al. *Mindfulness*. Piatkus, 2011.

Yerkes, R. M., and J. D. Dodson. "The relation of strength of stimulus to rapidity of habit-formation." *Journal of comparative neurology and psychology*, vol. 18, no. 5, 1908, pp. 459-482.

Zhuo, J. *The Making of a Manager: What to Do When Everyone Looks to You*. Ebury Publishing, 2019.

ABOUT THE AUTHOR

Flóra Raffai is a small organisation leader, trustee, and coach. Since 2015, she has been a Chief Executive Officer at small organisations, from a newly formed charity, a decades old awarding body, and a century old charity. She has served as a trustee and mentor for several small organisations, and is currently the Chair of Trustees at a Cambridge-based infrastructure charity.

Flóra is an accredited transformational coach, specialising in coaching small organisation leaders. She holds a BSc in International Relations from the London School of Economics, and a MSt in Social Innovation from the University of Cambridge Judge Business School.

Get in touch with Flóra by visiting https://www.rapport-coaching.com/.

Printed in Great Britain
by Amazon

58377777R00106